THE CIVIL WAR

SIEGE OF

JACKSON MISSISSIPPI

THE CIVIL WAR

SIEGE OF

JACKSON
MISSISSIPPI

JIM WOODRICK

FOREWORD BY TERRENCE J. WINSCHEL

THE
History
PRESS

Published by The History Press
Charleston, SC
www.historypress.net

First published 2016

ISBN 978-1-5402-1189-7

Library of Congress Control Number: 2015953414

Notice: The information in this book is true and complete to the best of our knowledge. It is offered without guarantee on the part of the author or The History Press. The author and The History Press disclaim all liability in connection with the use of this book.

In memory of Warren E. Grabau

CONTENTS

FOREWORD

The campaign for control of the Mississippi River was perhaps the most decisive of the Civil War and one of the more complex military operations in the nation's history. Waged over a thousand-mile front that stretched from Cairo, Illinois, to the Gulf of Mexico, the campaign pitted against one another significant land and naval forces of the North and South and included some of the war's most notable, colorful and even controversial figures.

Seared into the pages of history were the names of Grant, Sherman, Farragut, Porter, Beauregard, Albert Sidney Johnston and Joseph E. Johnston. Written in blood on those very same pages were names of places such as Fort Donelson, Shiloh and Vicksburg. The campaign culminated in July 1863, with the fall of the Confederate bastions at Vicksburg, Mississippi, on that "Glorious Fourth," and Port Hudson, Louisiana, on July 9. The final, yet seldom-mentioned, scene of the great drama was enacted in Jackson, the capital city of the Magnolia State, in which the enigmatic Southern general Joseph E. Johnston and the once proud Confederate Army of Relief was compelled to evacuate the city following a short-lived siege (July 10–17) by a Union expeditionary force led by William T. Sherman.

Other than a passing reference in association with the Vicksburg Campaign, the Siege of Jackson has garnered little attention in the ever-expanding field of literature on the Civil War. Only one short and hard-to-find volume, titled *The Battle of Jackson/The Siege of Jackson* (Baltimore, 1981) by Edwin C. Bearss and Warren Grabau, documents this siege in any detail.

Almost forty years later, historian Jim Woodrick shines a bright and powerful light on the Siege of Jackson and the men in blue and gray who experienced war in all its pageantry and tragedy under a broiling Mississippi sun. Written with great skill and passion by one whose intimacy with the subject has no peer, this smooth-flowing and fast-paced narrative details the Jackson siege with clarity and precision. The author highlights the human pathos of battle through scores of previously untapped sources that will captivate and enthrall readers across the broad spectrum from novice to expert. In this volume, Woodrick's mastery of the subject proves him worthy to document the Siege of Jackson, which stands equally worthy of his talented pen.

Terrence J. Winschel

ACKNOWLEDGEMENTS

A number of years ago, I was contacted by Warren Grabau, an eminent Civil War historian and author of *Ninety-Eight Days: A Geographer's View of the Vicksburg Campaign*, about the possibility of revising a book he co-authored with Edwin C. Bearss on the Battle and Siege of Jackson. Published in 1981 by the Jackson Civil War Round Table, it is the only book-length treatment on the role of Jackson during the Civil War. Needless to say, I was thrilled with the possibility of working with Warren and eagerly agreed. Unfortunately, it was not long afterward that Warren passed away. With his death, I lost a longtime friend and mentor, but the idea of a new book on Jackson stayed with me. Over time, I decided to focus on the Siege of Jackson as a stand-alone event, not only because it was of particular interest to me, but because it has received relatively little attention while the Battle of Jackson, fought in May 1863, has been covered fairly extensively as part of the overall Vicksburg Campaign. This book is the result of Warren's idea. I can only hope I have in some small measure lived up to his expectations.

It is a daunting task indeed to try to thank all those who have played a role in making this book a reality. I would be remiss in not making the attempt, however. First and foremost, I want to acknowledge the monumental work of Edwin C. Bearss, whose extensive knowledge and research on the Vicksburg Campaign and the Civil War in general is the foundation for this and many other published works. Along with Ed Bearss, there are a host of historians who have not only contributed to the growing number of books on the Vicksburg Campaign but who have generously provided advice and support.

ACKNOWLEDGEMENTS

In particular, I want to thank General Parker Hills and Terry Winschel for their willingness to share their encyclopedic knowledge and offer their sage advice throughout this project. Most of all, I value their kindness and warm friendship over the course of many years.

In compiling the information for this volume, I have had the pleasure of working with many wonderful people who have freely given of their time and resources. I am especially indebted to the staff of the Archives and Records Services Division of the Mississippi Department of Archives and History, particularly William Thompson and Jeff Giambrone; the Special Collections and Archives at the University of California, Riverside; the Special Collections Department of the McCain Library and Archives at the University of Southern Mississippi; Roberta Fairburn with the Abraham Lincoln Presidential Library in Springfield; Connie Langum, historian at the Wilson's Creek National Battlefield; Elizabeth Joyner, museum curator, Vicksburg National Military Park; George "Bubba" Bolm with the Old Court House Museum in Vicksburg; Captain William Carraway of South Carolina, who provided information on the history of the Twenty-sixth South Carolina Infantry; Shelby Harriel, Pearl River Community College, for information regarding the role of female soldiers at Jackson; Mary Woodward, chancellor of the Catholic Diocese of Jackson; Grady Howell, who seemingly knows all things related to Mississippi's Confederate soldiers; Todd Sanders, for his knowledge of antebellum resources in Jackson; Mark Farrell, who generously provided access to the Henry Tisdale diary; and all those unnamed individuals at libraries and other repositories who have taken the time to scan so many wonderful primary resources and make them available via the Internet. Your work is of incalculable benefit and much appreciated. Most of all, I want to thank Richard Dortch of Jackson, whose passion for history is infectious and who has been more than generous in sharing his copious research.

I also wish to thank my colleagues in the Historic Preservation Division of MDAH. Their dedication to the cause of historic preservation is far too often an underappreciated public service to the people of Mississippi. In particular, I want to thank Jennifer Baughn, whose thoughtful observations and keen advice have been a source of inspiration throughout.

To my editors at Arcadia Publishing and The History Press, especially Candice Lawrence, I appreciate your patience, understanding and encouragement.

And to my many friends at St. Columb's Episcopal Church in Ridgeland, I will perhaps never be able to express how much your interest in this project has meant to me. Even when you doubted this would ever come to fruition (and I *know* you did), you were at least kind enough not to say it too often or too loudly.

Finally, I am forever grateful for the support of my family—especially my wife, Mary Margaret—who has somehow managed to patiently live amid a growing mountain of books, papers and notes. Without her unwavering support, this book would have never been a reality.

INTRODUCTION

On the morning of July 3, 1863, Union soldiers along the siege lines at Vicksburg began noticing white flags popping up along the Confederate works. As more and more flags appeared, the firing ceased. For the first time since May 18, the guns were silent, and men in blue and gray took advantage of the stillness to emerge from the trenches. The cause of the sudden calm was a truce to consider terms for the surrender of fortress Vicksburg. To try to hammer out an agreement, Major General Ulysses S. Grant, commander of the besieging Union Army of the Tennessee, and Lieutenant General John C. Pemberton, the beleaguered Confederate general in charge of Vicksburg's defense, met underneath an oak tree between the lines. Although no agreement was reached until the next morning—the Fourth of July—the end was no longer in doubt. After forty-seven days of siege and more than a year of Federal operations to capture the city, Vicksburg was finally in Grant's pocket. The Confederate troops—threadbare and near starvation—marched out of their trenches and stacked arms. As a testimony to their valor, the victorious Union soldiers did not cheer their triumph, but few missed the significance of what had transpired. Not only had Vicksburg's surrender, coupled with the fall of Port Hudson, Louisiana, on July 9, resulted in the opening of the Mississippi River, but the Confederacy had been split in two. For the South, the loss of Vicksburg, combined with the defeat of Robert E. Lee's army at Gettysburg, was a devastating defeat from which there was little hope of recovery.[1]

As significant as the siege and surrender of Vicksburg was, however, it is only part of the story of what took place in Mississippi in the pivotal year of 1863. It was in reality the culmination of a long and complicated campaign. To fully appreciate Vicksburg's significance, one must understand the entire breadth of the campaign for control of the Mississippi River. Until recent years, the story of what is arguably the most important campaign of the Civil War generally played second fiddle to that of Gettysburg. Thanks to a number of dedicated historians, however—especially Edwin C. Bearss, Terry Winschel, Warren Grabau, Parker Hills, John Marszalek and Michael Ballard—the Vicksburg Campaign has finally gotten the attention it so readily deserves. As a result, battlefields and other important sites across a multi-state area are being studied, interpreted and visited with increased interest. Unfortunately, one of the battlefields associated with the Vicksburg Campaign has continued to be neglected: the Siege of Jackson.

Fought immediately after the surrender of Pemberton's army at Vicksburg, the Siege of Jackson has received scant attention. Unlike the Vicksburg National Military Park, where hundreds of monuments, markers and tablets dot the rolling landscape to mark the siege and defense lines, the battlefield at Jackson has disappeared over time. Like other urban battlefields, many of the sites associated with the siege have long since been paved over, and there are few physical reminders of the events that occurred in the summer of 1863. And unlike the Siege of Vicksburg, the conflict in Jackson ended without an exclamation mark. Rather than surrender his army, the Confederate commander at Jackson chose to abandon the city and save his army to fight another day. For these reasons, and perhaps others, the story of Jackson's Civil War siege has been largely forgotten. The men who fought and died here, however, deserve more.

For a week, more than seventy thousand men, blue and gray, fought under a hot Mississippi sun for control of Mississippi's capital city. Commanding the opposing forces were two men who would become quite familiar with each other as the war progressed. Defending the city was Confederate general Joseph E. Johnston, while Major General William Tecumseh Sherman led the Federal expeditionary force. Both men were graduates of West Point and, despite being on opposite sides, respected the other's ability. For Sherman, the expedition would prove to be his first successful independent command and went a long way in proving that he deserved to be among Grant's most trusted lieutenants. For Johnston, it was an ignominious end to the campaign in Mississippi. By surrendering Jackson, any hope of recapturing Vicksburg was lost forever.

During the weeklong siege, soldiers on both sides endured almost constant artillery bombardment, suffered from the sweltering heat and dodged the ever-present threat of sharpshooters. The fighting at Jackson also involved a desperate charge by a lone Union brigade, resulting in massive casualties. Afterward, the dead lay exposed in the unbearable heat until the Confederates asked for a truce to bury their remains. Outside the siege lines, the campaign included wide-ranging cavalry operations designed to inflict as much damage as possible to railroad facilities and other military installations throughout central Mississippi. Perhaps the most dramatic aspect of the siege, however, was the effect on the city itself. Briefly occupied by Union forces in May 1863, Jackson had already suffered damage by the time Sherman's army arrived in July. The destruction wrought during the siege and subsequent occupation by Union troops added more damage to what was once a thriving city. As a result, Jackson earned the unenviable nickname of "Chimneyville," a name that survives today.

In many ways, Jackson is the central figure in the drama that unfolded in July 1863. Established in 1821 as the Mississippi state capital, Jackson was, in essence, carved out of the wilderness. The town's primary significance was its geographical location, which was roughly in the center of the state. Although designated as the capital city, Jackson for many years had the look and feel of a rough frontier town, known perhaps more for its saloons than as the center of state government. As a result, other more populous and prosperous towns lobbied the Mississippi legislature to relocate the capital. Jackson's claim as the capital city was solidified, however, with the construction of a new statehouse, built in 1836–40. Designed by William Nichols, who was among the most prominent architects of the period, the state capitol (now known as the Old Capitol Museum) was easily the most prominent building in Jackson but was by no means the only one. Also designed by Nichols, the Governor's Mansion was constructed a few blocks west of the state capitol about 1840. Both buildings are today considered among the state's greatest architectural treasures.[2]

Other prominent, antebellum public buildings constructed helped transform Jackson from a frontier town into a real city. In 1847, work began on a city hall. The building served several functions, including use as an occasional concert and exhibition hall, and was home to two Masonic lodges, both meeting on the second floor. North of town, the Mississippi Insane Asylum, built by the same architect responsible for the city hall, was completed in 1855. An enormous structure, the asylum was considered in its day a model institution for the care of patients with mental illness. Located where the University of Mississippi Medical Center is today, the Insane Asylum survived into the twentieth century. An equally impressive state penitentiary building, yet another Nichols-designed structure, was located at the site of the present-day Mississippi state capitol, which was completed in 1903. West of town, located on the main road to Clinton, was the Deaf and Dumb Asylum, another of Mississippi's public institutions dedicated to the care and treatment of those in need. Unlike the Insane Asylum, the Deaf and Dumb Asylum did not survive the Civil War.[3]

Along with its public buildings, Jackson had a full complement of retail, commercial and industrial establishments by 1860. Most of the shops and larger stores were located along the southern end of State Street and specialized in a wide variety of goods, including drugs, ready-made clothes, farm implements, jewelry and musical instruments. Between Pearl and Pascagoula Streets was an area known as "Cheapside" where a number of general stores were located. Farther down State Street near the Southern Railroad depot were buildings dedicated to a different sort of trade: both the W.A. Showalter and the Harris, Skidmore & Co. sold slaves. Other establishments, most of them clustered within a couple blocks of the capitol building, offered an impressive assortment of entertainments, including a number of restaurants and saloons. Occupying one of the most prominent corner lots in the city, at the corner of Capitol and State Streets, was the firm of Spengler & Zehnder, which offered for sale "Cigars, Tobacco, Fruit and Fancy Articles." By far the most numerous type of establishment, however, were law offices. In 1860, more than thirty lawyers had offices in Jackson, most located in close proximity to the capitol.[4]

Jackson's antebellum economy also included several manufacturing concerns. Before the war, the city boasted a cotton mill, a foundry, a carriage and buggy factory, a marble works, blacksmiths, gun makers, bookbinders and a frame emporium. Along with these commercial and manufacturing enterprises, there were several hotels and boardinghouses in operation, the most prominent of which was the Bowman House hotel, a four-story brick building located north of the capitol on the east side of State Street. Known as Mississippi's "largest and most commodious hotel," the Bowman House opened its doors in 1857. A couple of blocks west was the Jackson House, while "Mrs. Dickson's" welcomed guests at the corner of West and Pearl Streets. In all, Jackson boasted ten hotels or boardinghouses where travelers could rent rooms and get a bite to eat. There were six churches, too, including Baptist, Methodist, Christian, Episcopal, Presbyterian and Catholic congregations. There was also a Jewish presence, though Jackson's first synagogue was not constructed until 1866. By all accounts, Jackson was a booming place just prior to the Civil War, although the population did not exceed 3,500, slave and free.[5]

While Jackson's citizens had worked hard to create a prosperous business environment, it was the arrival of the railroads that really put the city on the map. As early as 1840, a rail line was established from Jackson to Vicksburg, connecting the capital city with the Mississippi River. A decade later, rail service was established east to Brandon, including a much-needed bridge across the Pearl. In 1856, a north–south line connected Jackson with Canton, located about twenty miles north, and two years after that, the New Orleans, Jackson and Great Northern Railroad (NOJ&GN) linked Jackson and the Crescent City. The final rail link occurred in 1861, when the Southern Railroad of Mississippi completed construction of its line all the way east to Meridian. With railroads radiating in all directions, Jackson became an important crossroads town. This, of course, would also make Jackson a tempting military target.[6]

In addition to Jackson's military value, the capital city was also a political target, as it was the site of Mississippi's secession in 1861 and the seat of Mississippi's Confederate government. On January 7, 1861, one hundred delegates convened at the state capitol to consider whether to leave the Union, a move strongly favored by Governor John Jones Pettus. Two days later, on January 9, the delegates voted 84–15 in favor of secession, joining South Carolina, which voted to secede on December 20, 1860. With a large crowd packing the gallery of the house chamber to witness the historic vote and hundreds more waiting outside, Jackson's Methodist minister, the Reverend Whitfield Harrington, offered a prayer for the "new-born Republic." His prayer, according to Governor Pettus, was "offered in the most fervent and impressive manner to the great Ruler of Nations." Before the assembled throng, Harrington called on Almighty God to pour out his blessings upon the Republic of Mississippi and asked that "her name become the synonym of courage and patriotism among the nations of the earth" and that the Southern states, united in their cause, "be guided by Thy providence to that part of virtue where the storm of human passions hush their fury and the billows that rock Republics to ruin subside in peaceful tranquility forever." After the prayer, the crowd broke into wild celebration amid the "roaring of cannon, the ringing of bells and other demonstrations of joy." Any idea that "peaceful tranquility" would abound, however, was shattered with the firing on Fort Sumter in Charleston's harbor on April 12. The Civil War had begun, and with it the fate of Mississippi and Jackson hung in the balance.[7]

CHAPTER 1

"THE EYES AND HOPES OF THE WHOLE CONFEDERACY ARE UPON YOU"

On the night of May 13, 1863, Joseph E. Johnston settled into his room at the Bowman House hotel in Jackson. Although the Bowman House was considered the finest in the city, the fifty-six-year-old Virginian was not there to enjoy the accommodations. In fact, he had just arrived by train that night amid a truly chaotic scene. Despite a pouring rain, Jackson's citizens clogged the streets in a desperate attempt to leave the city. On the way, Johnston had received a telegram from Lieutenant General John C. Pemberton in Vicksburg with the alarming news that Union forces under Ulysses S. Grant were moving swiftly into the interior of the state, news that sent the citizens of Mississippi's capital into an uproar. Despite the bravado of the local newspaper, which had boasted just three days earlier that "the enemy will never reach Jackson," it was obvious to most that the situation had taken a decided turn for the worse. And while Governor John Pettus exhorted in vain for his fellow Mississippians to "join your brothers in arms, your sons and neighbors who are now baring their bosoms to the storm of battle at your very doors," the state government was already in the process of evacuating the city. It was into this maelstrom that Joseph E. Johnston arrived on the evening of May 13. He had come to Jackson to restore order, but not necessarily by choice. In fact, Johnston had been ordered to Mississippi by Confederate secretary of war James A. Seddon to take command and give the troops defending the area "the encouragement and benefit of your personal direction." It would be a Herculean task.[8]

On paper, Johnston was a logical choice. Born in Virginia in 1807, Joseph Eggleston Johnston graduated from West Point in 1829 ranked thirteenth in his class. From then until the outbreak of the Civil War, Johnston served almost continuously in the army and was wounded during both the Seminole Wars and the Mexican War. In 1855, he became a lieutenant colonel with the First United States Cavalry and was then appointed as the army's quartermaster general in June 1860, with a brigadier general's rank. This seemingly plumb assignment might be attributable to his marriage in 1845 to Lydia McLane, whose father was a former congressman and secretary of the treasury and secretary of state, but it also spoke well of

Confederate general Joseph E. Johnston. *Library of Congress.*

Johnston's organizational skills. When Virginia decided to cast its lot with the Confederate States of America the next year, however, Johnston followed, despite his prominent post in the U.S. Army. Within a matter of months, he obtained a brigadier general's rank in the new government and would have—perhaps should have—become the highest ranking officer in the new army. Unfortunately for Johnston, President Jefferson Davis, for a variety of reasons, decided to place Johnston fourth on the list of ranking generals. This slight, at least from Johnston's viewpoint, would be the source of bitter feelings between Johnston and Davis. Over time, that bitterness grew into a deep mistrust between the two men.[9]

Despite this, Johnston was given command of the Confederate forces in Virginia early in the war and was the ranking officer at the Battle of First Manassas. With that signal victory, it is likely that Johnston would have ascended to command what would become the Army of Northern Virginia. However, he was grievously wounded at the battle of Seven Pines in May 1862, and during his six-month recovery, Robert E. Lee took Johnston's place at the head of that army. By the time Johnston returned to duty in November, Davis decided to send him to the western theater to command a far-flung department that included armies in both Tennessee and Mississippi. A difficult assignment, given the amount of territory he was expected to defend, Johnston's task would be all the more difficult because of the personalities involved. Commanding the Army of Tennessee was General Braxton Bragg, a glowering and brooding officer whose relationship with his own subordinates was rocky at best. In Mississippi, Johnston relied on John Clifford Pemberton, a native of Pennsylvania. While a competent officer, some of Pemberton's subordinates suspected his allegiance to the Confederate cause. To complicate matters, both Bragg and Pemberton received regular communications from Davis directly, and the president's directives were often in conflict with those of Johnston's. All these factors contributed to a clumsy and often stormy arrangement that was hardly a recipe for success in Mississippi or in middle Tennessee, where Johnston chose to remain to keep an eye on Bragg. Despite these challenges, Seddon sent orders to Johnston to report to Jackson on May 9. He arrived in the middle of the night in a pouring rain, accompanied by his staff and personal physician.[10]

Almost immediately after arriving at the Bowman House, Johnston was briefed by Brigadier General John Gregg, whose brigade of Tennessee and Texas troops fought an all-day battle on May 12 near the village of Raymond, located approximately fifteen miles southwest of Jackson. Gregg's brigade had arrived in Jackson by rail from Port Hudson with 3,000 men and then quickly marched to Raymond, determined to ambush what he thought was an isolated Union brigade operating on Grant's right flank. After reaching Raymond, Gregg positioned his men behind Fourteenmile Creek and waited for the enemy. Instead of a single brigade, however, it turned out to be Union major general James B. McPherson's entire XVII Corps, which was on the march toward Raymond. Gregg, however, had no idea he faced such odds and ordered his men on the offensive. Attacking with savage fury, Gregg initially had success, but the preponderance of numbers eventually forced his badly outnumbered brigade

Confederate lieutenant general John C. Pemberton. *Library of Congress.*

back. After six hours of heavy combat, Gregg retreated toward Jackson, where he was joined by Brigadier General W.H.T. Walker's brigade, which had just arrived from Savannah, Georgia. The affair at Raymond cost Gregg's brigade 73 killed, 252 wounded and 190 missing, but the fight had far greater impact than that. As a result of the fighting at Raymond, Grant pivoted his army toward Jackson with the weight of two Union corps, determined to eliminate whatever threat Johnston might pose before turning west toward Vicksburg. It was a bold move, and one neither Pemberton nor Johnston would be able to effectively counter.[11]

In his meeting with Johnston, Gregg reported that there were approximately six thousand men on hand to defend Jackson and that troops under the aptly named Brigadier General States Rights Gist were scheduled to arrive soon from Charleston, South Carolina. He also reported, rather alarmingly, that as many as twenty-five thousand Federals under Major General William Tecumseh Sherman were at Clinton, just ten miles or so west of Jackson. This was in error; in fact, there were two divisions of McPherson's corps at Clinton while Sherman, unbeknownst to either Gregg or Johnston, was at Mississippi Springs and moving north toward Jackson. Regardless, the news that Grant's army was already so close to Jackson and

On May 12, Gregg's brigade fought the Union XVII Corps at the battle of Raymond. *Illustrations by Theodore R. Davis. Library of Congress.*

was positioned between his army and Pemberton's was of grave concern to Johnston. Coupled with word that the fortifications that had recently been erected around Jackson were inferior, Johnston was convinced that holding the city would be impossible and immediately wired Seddon that he "had arrived this evening, finding the enemy's force between this place and General Pemberton, cutting off communication." Johnston closed his report with these words: "I am too late."[12]

Based on the information provided to him, Johnston began sending messages to Pemberton to march toward Jackson and attack Sherman (presumably at Clinton) from the west while Johnston would cooperate with the troops he had available from the east. Upon receipt of these orders on the morning of May 14, Pemberton was alarmed at the idea of abandoning Vicksburg in order to coordinate an attack with Johnston. For Pemberton, holding Vicksburg was the primary goal of the troops under his command and he was supported in this belief by Jefferson Davis, who had stated that Vicksburg was "the nail head that holds the South's two halves together."[13] As such, Davis would under no circumstance approve any plan to abandon Vicksburg, yet this is precisely what Johnston now ordered Pemberton to do. Caught between a veritable rock and a hard place, Pemberton chose to ignore Johnston's order and instead called a council of war, where his two senior division commanders encouraged him instead to attack Grant's supply line by moving to the southeast and astride the road between Raymond and Grand Gulf. This, of course, would mean moving farther away from Johnston's force. After choosing this option and putting his army into motion, Pemberton abruptly changed his mind en route and tried to turn his army around after receiving another missive from Johnston to unite their forces at Clinton. Before Pemberton was able to move very far, however, Grant caught up with him at Champion Hill near Edwards. As a result of the bloody fighting there on May 16, Pemberton's army was almost annihilated and forced to retreat toward Vicksburg. Had Pemberton somehow been successful in reaching Clinton, it would not have satisfied Johnston's directive anyway. By the time the guns of Champion Hill sounded, Johnston had long since abandoned Jackson and was moving north, farther and farther away from Pemberton.[14]

After sending the message to Richmond that he had arrived "too late," Johnston made arrangements to remove supplies and public property to Canton. At the same time, he ordered Gregg to fight a delaying action to provide sufficient time to complete the withdrawal. Responding with alacrity, Gregg had his troops on the move at 3:00 a.m. Marching out about three miles west of town in a pouring rain, the Confederates established a defensive position at a farm owned by Oliver Perry Wright (near the present-day Jackson Zoo). Here, a brigade-sized force under the command of Colonel Peyton Colquitt, which included Captain James A. Hoskin's Brookhaven (Mississippi) Light Artillery, waited for the expected Union advance. The rain continued to pelt down, turning the roads into mud. That, as it happened, was good fortune for Johnston, as McPherson's XVII Corps was slowed in its advance on Jackson. By 9:00 a.m., however, the forward elements of Brigadier General Marcellus M.

Confederate brigadier general John Gregg. *DeGolyer Library, Southern Methodist University.*

Crocker's division encountered Colquitt's roadblock, and Hoskin's guns went into action. For some time, the two sides traded artillery fire until the bottom dropped out. Unable to move forward in the heavy rain, McPherson's men waited. Meanwhile, Sherman's XV Corps, accompanied by Grant, had been marching undetected toward Jackson from Mississippi Springs. Finally alerted by scouts that the Federals were moving up on two fronts, Gregg quickly shifted some of his reserves to cover the crossing of Lynch Creek south of the city. Sherman's vanguard, consisting of Brigadier General James M. Tuttle's division, approached the creek to find Confederate artillery in place on the opposite side. Here, Colonel Albert P. Thompson's Third Kentucky Mounted Infantry opened fire as Tuttle's division began to deploy, but the contest was short-lived. Heavily outnumbered, Thompson's men fell back into the earthworks that had been erected and waited for the Federals to advance. It was a little after 11:00 a.m.[15]

On the western edge of the city, the violent rainstorm finally eased, and McPherson's troops advanced against Colquitt's position. After a brief but sharp fight, which included a hand-to-hand struggle between the Tenth Missouri (U.S.) and the Twenty-fourth South Carolina Infantry, Colquitt was forced to withdraw into the main earthworks, located near the modern-day intersection of Capitol and Monument Streets. After lobbing a few shells into

Fighting occurred at the O.P. Wright farm on May 14 during the battle of Jackson. *Sketch by A.E. Matthews, Thirty-first Ohio Volunteer Infantry. Library of Congress.*

the Federal lines and forcing McPherson's men to deploy, Gregg ordered his men to retreat, as he had received word that the supplies were now safely on the road to Canton. He also alerted Thompson to withdraw his troops to the north, leaving enough gun crews in place to delay Sherman's advance. These men, along with a number of sharpshooters, were subsequently captured by Union troops.[16]

After withdrawing from Jackson, Gregg's men marched approximately seven miles north to Tougaloo, where they bivouacked for the night. With Jackson abandoned by Johnston's troops, the capital city was quickly occupied by the Federals. Upon entering the city, the national colors of the Fifty-ninth Indiana were hoisted above the state capitol, and Grant, along with McPherson and Sherman, met in the Bowman House. Here, they planned the army's next movements, which would involve marching swiftly to the west to prevent the junction of the two Confederate armies, unaware that Pemberton and Johnston were at this point moving away from each other. After drafting orders for the next day's movements, Grant instructed Sherman to begin destroying Jackson's railroads and "all the property belonging to the enemy." At that, Grant retired for the night to the same room that Johnston had used the night before. It is likely that Grant slept more soundly than Johnston.[17]

Before Sherman got to bed, he drafted orders appointing Brigadier General Joseph Mower as the garrison commander in Jackson and designating his brigade as the provost guard. Mower, described as "[a] bout six feet in height, well-proportioned and of great physical strength," established his headquarters at the state capitol, and his brigade, which included the Eighth Wisconsin Infantry, the mascot of which was "Old Abe" the eagle, occupied the grounds. Tuttle and Major General Frederick Steele, commanding two of Sherman's divisions, were ordered to begin destroying the railroads the next morning. McPherson's XVII Corps camped in the vicinity of the Deaf and Dumb Asylum, and the men marched out the next morning after replenishing their haversacks with provisions obtained primarily from the state penitentiary, which had been converted into a munitions factory after the start of the war.[18]

By 10:00 a.m. on the fifteenth, the destruction of the railroads began in earnest. The method used to destroy the tracks involved prying the rails up, heating them over a pile of railroad ties and then bending the heated rails around a tree or other object. Once bent, the twisted rails resembled a gentleman's cravat, earning them the nickname "Sherman's neckties." This method would be repeated during the second occupation of Jackson two months later and would become standard operating procedure during the Atlanta Campaign and the March to the Sea in 1864. In addition to the railroads, the depots and railroad bridge across the Pearl River were torched. The damage to the railroads wrought by Sherman's troops was extensive and would not be fully repaired until after the war, but the damage to the city itself, despite the presence of guards ostensibly to protect private property, was also extensive.

Grant's order to Sherman to destroy "all property belonging to the enemy" was meant to include the various factories and depots scattered about the city for the benefit of the Confederate war effort. These included a textile factory located near the depot for the Southern Railroad owned by two brothers, Joshua and Thomas Green. On the morning of the fifteenth, Grant and Sherman visited the factory and observed tent cloth stamped "C.S.A." in production, with the workers (mostly young women) still at the looms. Frantically appealing to the two generals that loss of his business would leave the workers unemployed, the Green brothers soon saw their factory go up in flames. In addition to the textile mill, the Federals burned an iron foundry, two cotton mills, a covered bridge (which had at one time served as a temporary prison for captured Union soldiers), a carriage factory (converted to producing limbers and caissons) and the state penitentiary.

Other buildings also went up in flames, though not connected to the war effort, including a block of businesses located near city hall, as well as the Catholic church, which was located on Court Street. According to a soldier in the Eighth Wisconsin, much of the damage was the result of a company of Indians from the Fifth Minnesota. "No sooner had they comprehended the nature of the work we had to do," he wrote, "than they 'put their war paint on,' and with demoniac yells and all sorts of leapings and wild motions began putting the torch to every house they came to—dwelling houses, churches, stables, etc."[19] The fires and widespread looting by Union troops went on despite Sherman's admonition to Mower that "only such articles should be taken as are necessary to the subsistence of troops" and that the soldiers should respect the private rights of citizens. "The feeling of pillage and booty will injure the morals of the troops," Sherman concluded, "and bring disgrace on our cause." It should be noted, however, that no action was taken to punish those who participated in the looting and burning of private property.[20]

By abandoning Jackson as quickly as he had, Johnston failed to give time for additional reinforcements to reach him. These troops might have given him enough men to mount a proper defense of the city, although Grant's quick reaction in rushing two corps to Jackson might have doomed the effort from the start. The rest of Gist's brigade, for example, reached Brandon on May 14. Brigadier General Samuel B. Maxey's brigade, meanwhile, was en route from Port Hudson and had reached Hazlehurst when the station master handed Maxey a telegram from Brigadier General John Adams warning him not to move any farther north. Adams closed the message by announcing that "we are evacuating Jackson." This news struck Maxey like a thunderbolt, as this was the first indication he had that Jackson was in any danger. Not trusting the veracity of the telegram, Maxey sent a locomotive forward with a member of his staff and the railroad superintendent aboard to see what they could discover. Six miles below Jackson, they encountered another messenger aboard a hand car, who carried an order from Johnston for Maxey to "take measures to save your command by crossing Pearl River and going to the Southern Railroad, unless you can find a more judicious move." The message also indicated that other troops were on the east side of the Pearl (meaning Gist's brigade, which had similarly been warned away from advancing any farther). Convinced that Jackson was no longer an option, Maxey returned to Brookhaven with his brigade. It would take nine days for his brigade to finally enter Jackson, by which time the Federals had long since marched west to begin investing Vicksburg.[21]

Why Johnston did not attempt to mount a defense of Jackson in May is still a subject of debate, but in hindsight, it was probably a wise decision. Even with the addition of Gist's and Maxey's brigades, Johnston would still have been heavily outnumbered, and many of these troops had suffered from an extensive and exhausting trek by rail. However, Johnston did not know that he faced such odds when he wired Seddon on the evening of May 13 that he was "too late." At that point, the information provided by Gregg indicated that there were just two divisions of Union infantry at Clinton. With reinforcements close at hand, Johnston should have calculated that he would have enough for a defensive stand. By deciding to evacuate Jackson before any of these reinforcements arrived, it is clear Johnston never intended to defend the capital city. In addition, by retreating northeast toward Canton, despite constantly urging Pemberton to unite their forces, it would appear that Johnston had no real intention of fighting a pitched battle with Grant's troops anytime soon, certainly not until Johnston was satisfied that he had enough men on hand to have a chance of success. The question, in the coming days and weeks, would be when—or perhaps if—he would ever have enough men to relieve Vicksburg.

After the battle of Jackson on May 14 and the subsequent occupation of the city by Federal troops, Grant and Pemberton collided at Champion Hill on May 16. Barely averting complete disaster, Pemberton managed to fall back into the defenses at Vicksburg. To allow Loring's division time to cross the Big Black River, however, Pemberton established a blocking force on the east side of the river near the railroad crossing. On May 17, Grant smashed this force as well in a brief but decisive battle. Loring's division had never appeared and had subsequently been separated from the main force. By the time the first Union troops began arriving in front of Vicksburg itself, Johnston was in Vernon in northwest Madison County, where he sent a request to Richmond for "very large re-enforcements" to relieve Vicksburg. In response, the authorities in Richmond promised "all aids and facilities in the power of the Department to render" but also cautioned Johnston that they would likely be less than he hoped.

As promised, reinforcements began pouring into central Mississippi from the far-flung corners of the Confederacy. By the third week of May, Gist's troops had been joined by Brigadier General Evander McNair's brigade and Brigadier General Matthew Ector's brigade, consisting of four Texas regiments. McNair's and Ector's men had been transferred from the Army of Tennessee. Combined with Gist's brigade, these reinforcements increased the number of troops available to Johnston to more than eleven thousand.

Gist's, Ector's and McNair's brigades, numbering perhaps five thousand men, arrived in Livingston on May 20 and went into camp. Accompanying these men as they marched north from Jackson was a British observer, an officer with Her Majesty's Coldstream Guards. Marching with the column, Lieutenant Colonel Arthur Freemantle observed that the "straggling of the Georgians was on the grandest scale conceivable." Arriving in Madison County, Freemantle took the opportunity to visit Johnston, whose headquarters was several miles southwest of Canton. He described Johnston as "rather below middle height, spare, soldierlike, and well set up; his features are good, and

Confederate brigadier general Evander McNair. *Library of Congress.*

he has lately taken to wear a grayish beard." Johnston, he wrote, appeared "calm, deliberate, and confident," and he noted that his only cooking utensils were "an old coffeepot and frying pan—both very inferior articles. There was only one fork (one prong deficient) between himself and staff, and this was handed to me ceremoniously as the 'guest.'"[22]

The same day these reinforcements arrived in Livingston, Loring's division, which had been wandering around after being separated from Pemberton's army at Champion Hill, finally stumbled into Jackson. Along the way, most of the division's supplies had been lost, including, according to a soldier in the Fifteenth Mississippi, "our artillery, wagons, knapsacks, blankets, and everything we had."[23] As a result, they arrived in Jackson in need of food, cooking utensils and, in some cases, rifles. As the nearly five-thousand-man division marched into town, the people of Jackson welcomed the long gray column with open arms. "As we marched along the street," recalled Albert T. Goodloe, a soldier in the Thirty-fifth Alabama, "buckets of water were brought to us by the citizens, who also handed us large quantities of the best quality of chewing tobacco."[24] With Loring in Jackson, Johnston divided his force into two wings, assigning Loring command of the force at Jackson and the right wing, headquartered in Canton, under the command of Gist. Johnston, as overall commander of the "Army of Relief," planned to shuttle back and forth between the wings. While Johnston was rearranging his command, Pemberton's army was fighting for its life, repelling a grand assault by Grant's army on May 22.

Brigadier General Nathan G. "Shanks" Evans's brigade was the next to arrive in Jackson. Stationed at James Island, South Carolina, Evans's brigade included five South Carolina infantry regiments, plus the Holcombe Legion and an artillery battery. After boarding a train in Charleston on May 16, Evans's brigade arrived after a weeklong journey and was added to Loring's wing. With these arrivals, Johnston's army grew to more than twenty-two thousand men. On May 30, Johnston decided to shift Loring's wing to Canton. Early the next morning, Loring marched his men north of Jackson and boarded the train above the place where the line had been destroyed on May 15. With Loring's division and Maxey's brigade in Canton, Johnston's right wing, now under the command of W.H.T. Walker, marched to Yazoo City, where they arrived on June 1.[25]

Left to guard Jackson after Loring's departure was a single brigade, that of Evans's South Carolinians. On the first day of June, however, Major General John C. Breckinridge's division of 5,200 men arrived, adding significant firepower and experience to Johnston's growing force. His division had been ordered to Mississippi by Braxton Bragg at the behest of President Davis. Departing on May 24, it took a week for Breckinridge's division to arrive. Along the way, some of the "Orphans" were involved in a train derailment west of Meridian, killing several men. Upon his arrival in Jackson, Breckinridge assumed command of all the troops in the city and called on Governor Pettus to provide work crews to help improve the city's defenses. According to Breckinridge, the work was necessary because "time is blood now."[26]

Two days after Breckinridge's arrival, Johnston received the last of the reinforcements sent to him to relieve Vicksburg. Unlike the troops that had been shuttled to Mississippi via the railroad, Brigadier General William H. "Red" Jackson's cavalry division—more than three thousand men—had marched overland from Spring Hill, Tennessee. Arriving in Canton, Jackson's division went into camp east of town on the Sharon Road. With the addition of these mounted troops, Johnston now had more than thirty thousand men, which should have been enough to begin some sort of operation to relieve Pemberton.[27] Johnston, however, continued to call for more reinforcements. Exasperated, Seddon wrote back on June 5, "I regret inability to promise more troops, as we have drained resources even to the point of danger of several points." Citing needs in Virginia, Seddon flatly stated, "You must rely on what you have and the irregular forces Mississippi can afford." When Johnston protested ten days later that "saving Vicksburg is hopeless," Seddon, clearly losing his patience, emphasized that Vicksburg "must not be lost without a desperate struggle. The interest and honor of the Confederacy forbid it." He wrote, "I rely on you still to avert the loss. If better resources do not offer, you must hazard attack." Instead of moving Johnston to take the offensive, however, the war of words continued. On June 18, Johnston replied that he could not attack Grant because the Big Black River would cut off any hope of retreat in case of a defeat. In response, Seddon, using a bit of psychology with Johnston, first praised his abilities as a commander and stated that he deferred to Johnston's "judgement and military genius" to choose the right course of action. However, Seddon then reminded Johnston that "the eyes and hopes of the whole Confederacy are upon you, with the full confidence that you will act, and with the sentiment that it were better to fail nobly daring than through prudence even to be inactive."[28]

While Johnston lobbied for reinforcements, the beleaguered Vicksburg garrison watched and waited for any sign that he would come to their rescue. Meanwhile, Johnston's troops were scattered at various camps throughout the region between Jackson and the east bank of the Big Black River. Despite the hot weather, many of the soldiers in the "Army of Relief" found their stay quite comfortable. Robert Patrick of the Fourth Louisiana Infantry recalled that the regiment's camp at Beattie's Bluff was "a splendid camping place, being a lovely and retired grassy plot, covered with luxuriant grass, perfectly level, and having on three sides large and noble forest trees, and there was a splendid spring of water that afforded a good supply." Major Khleber Van Zandt of the Seventh Texas Infantry, on the other hand, reported that he and his men had not slept under a tent since leaving Port Hudson and had been "going all the time." Still, he wrote, "Our men have borne their hardships finely and nobly."[29]

On June 11, it appeared that Johnston might finally be ready to move, as he ordered Walker's division to shift from Yazoo City to the east side of the Big Black in anticipation of a march toward Vicksburg. By the fifteenth, Walker's troops arrived at Vernon, where they joined Loring's wing while Breckinridge remained in Jackson. On the same day that Walker's men arrived, however, Johnston received a telegram from Richmond informing him that significant reinforcements had also been sent to Grant. This intelligence, sent to Johnston directly from President Davis, had the immediate effect of halting any plans for a forward movement. As a result, Johnston wrote Pemberton that he was "too weak" to come to his assistance, and for the next

Union major general William Tecumseh Sherman. *Library of Congress.*

couple of weeks he did nothing. All the while, the siege lines continued to tighten around Pemberton.[30]

The intelligence handed to Johnston was correct. While Johnston marked time, Grant's besieging army received significant reinforcements. Drawing troops from across the region—the most significant addition was the arrival of the IX Corps from Kentucky on June 17—Grant now had approximately seventy-seven thousand men. Although Johnston and Pemberton's troops, if combined, briefly outnumbered Grant's, the advantage had shifted in Grant's favor by the middle of June. With the "Army of Relief" gathering strength east of the Big Black, Grant wanted to ensure that Johnston would be unable to come to Pemberton's rescue. To guard against any threat from Johnston, Grant shifted a significant number of these reinforcements to an exterior line facing the Big Black and covering an area known as the Mechanicsburg Corridor north of Vicksburg. These troops, consisting of seven Union divisions, were commanded by William Tecumseh Sherman.[31]

Born in 1820 in Lancaster, Ohio, Sherman was one of eleven children. When his father died at an early age, Sherman went to live with Thomas Ewing, an influential U.S. senator, and he eventually married Ewing's daughter. After graduating from West Point in 1840, Sherman spent several years in the army out West, including service in the Mexican War (although he saw no action). In 1853, he resigned his commission to enter the banking business and then tried his hand at law. Both ventures failed. In 1859, he became superintendent of the Louisiana State Seminary of Learning and Military Education (predecessor to Louisiana State University), where he remained until 1861. At that point, he returned north and secured an appointment as colonel of the Thirteenth U.S. Infantry. After fighting at the Battle of First Manassas, Sherman rose quickly in rank and was promoted to major general in May 1862. Throughout the Vicksburg Campaign, he successfully led the XV Corps and was among Grant's most trusted lieutenants, despite leading a failed attack at Chickasaw Bayou north of Vicksburg in December 1862. Grant and Sherman had clearly established a relationship based on mutual trust; as such, it was Sherman whom Grant entrusted with the protection of his army from Johnston.[32]

By late June, all of Sherman's troops were securely in place behind extensive fortifications extending from Snyder's Bluff overlooking the Yazoo River on the northern (left) flank, to the high ground west of Messinger's Ferry on the Big Black River near the southern (right) flank. Messinger's crossing was protected by both infantry and artillery while cavalry pickets stood watch over the crossings at Jones's Ford, Birdsong's Ferry and Bush's Ferry north of Messinger's and the Bridgeport, Coaker's Ferry and Hooker's Ferry crossings south of Messinger's. The southern end of Sherman's line terminated with Brigadier General Peter J. Osterhaus's division guarding the bluffs above the burned-out Southern Railroad bridge crossing, where a temporary bridge was in place. To provide for rapid communication, Grant had telegraph lines strung along his interior lines.[33]

It was not until the first of July that Johnston finally started moving toward the Big Black. Within days of the order to march, four Confederate divisions were in position at or near the river. Walker's and Loring's divisions were positioned near Birdsong's Ferry, as well as a division assigned to Major General Samuel French, who had been on leave visiting his home in the Mississippi Delta since reporting to Jackson on June 10. Finally arriving at Johnston's headquarters on July 3, French met with the other division commanders and then took charge of a division that included Maxey's, McNair's and Evans's brigades.

Breckinridge's division, meanwhile, was at Edwards, within a short march of the Big Black River railroad crossing. After probing Sherman's outer defenses, however, Johnston became convinced that the exterior Union line was simply too strong to effect a crossing of the river north of the Southern Railroad. As such, he decided to move south of the railroad with the bulk of his army and look for an undefended crossing there. It was too late for any such move, however, as Pemberton, unable to hold out any longer, surrendered the Vicksburg garrison on the Fourth of July. Now Johnston, instead of moving to the attack, would be pulling his army back in the face of an aggressive foe moving east toward Jackson.[34]

CHAPTER 2

"THE COUNTRY EXPECTS...THAT EVERY MAN WILL DO HIS DUTY"

Aware that the Confederates were in dire straits in Vicksburg, Grant had already been discussing plans for going after Johnston with Sherman's troops. On July 3, about the time Johnston's men finally arrived on the east bank of the Big Black, Sherman received a telegram from Grant notifying him that Pemberton had asked to discuss terms of surrender. While Grant indicated that he could not yet agree to the terms proposed, it was obvious that the siege was close to an end and Grant wanted Sherman to be ready to move at once. "I want Johnston broken up as effectually as possible, and [rail] roads destroyed," Grant wrote, and Sherman agreed. "Telegraph me the moment you have Vicksburg in possession," he replied, "and I will secure all the crossings...and move on Jackson or Canton, as you may advise." Although he had much work to do to get his troops ready, Sherman allowed himself a brief moment of celebration for the fall of Vicksburg, proclaiming it "the best Fourth of July since 1776."[35]

Grant sent another telegram later that day outlining his desire that Sherman not only attack Johnston but wreck the New Orleans, Jackson and Great Northern Railroad north and south of Jackson. Meanwhile, Sherman worked feverously to develop his plans for the upcoming campaign. To ensure success, Sherman requested another six divisions from the remainder of the XIII Corps and XV Corps still in the trenches at Vicksburg. Grant approved the request and issued orders that night for the men of the XIII Corps, commanded by Major General Edward O.C. Ord, and Sherman's own XV Corps, currently led by Major General Frederick Steele, to join Sherman as soon as Vicksburg's surrender was official. Thus, these men, who had endured forty-seven days of siege operations, would receive no rest or satisfaction in seeing the city they had worked so hard to capture. Instead, they would be called on to move at a moment's notice. A soldier in Colonel Daniel Lindsey's brigade of Osterhaus's division remembered that the men were "not sorry to be out of the broiling trenches" but expressed disappointment that they would not get to experience the end of the siege. "All felt that Vicksburgh was surely ours," he wrote, "and there was a pang of regret in the thought that after all the hard fighting of the past six months we should not be in at the death." Despite the regret experienced by many soldiers, much work was ahead for the veterans of the Vicksburg siege.[36]

Union major general John G. Parke, commander of the IX Corps. *Library of Congress.*

Also reinforcing Sherman from the investing lines at Vicksburg were the two divisions of the IX Corps. Unlike the bulk of Grant's army, these men were almost entirely from the eastern seaboard states and had only recently been transferred to Mississippi. Not only did these men have to endure the harsh summer heat, as eastern troops, they were often considered less than ideal soldiers by the veterans from the "western" states of Illinois, Indiana, Ohio, Michigan, Iowa, Wisconsin and Missouri. Commanded by Major General John Grubb Parke, the IX Corps units, with the exception of five Michigan regiments, all hailed from Pennsylvania, New Hampshire, New York, Massachusetts and Rhode Island. They had much to prove in the coming days. Parke himself was a Pennsylvanian. A West Point graduate, Parke was a topographical engineer. After promotion to major general in August 1862, he served as Ambrose Burnside's chief of staff during the Antietam and Fredericksburg Campaigns before elevation to corps command.[37] Despite his experience in the eastern theater, there was surely some trepidation on the part of his western counterparts when his corps

arrived in Mississippi during the Siege of Vicksburg, but his troops would earn their stripes during the upcoming campaign. To provide strength to the IX Corps, Sherman added Brigadier General William Sooy Smith's division of the XV Corps, composed entirely of "western" men.

To begin the move against Jackson, Sherman first had to cross the Big Black River, which was guarded in several places by Johnston's Confederates. To accomplish the crossing, Sherman planned to concentrate his army at three places: Messinger's Ferry, Birdsong's Ferry and the Big Black River Bridge. As soon as word reached Sherman that Vicksburg had officially surrendered, he sent orders to his corps commanders to begin moving. Steele's XV Corps was directed to march to Messinger's Ferry by way of the Bridgeport Road. Ord's XIII Corps was instructed to move to the Big Black River Bridge, where they would be joined by Brigadier General John McArthur's XVII Corps division, which would remain to guard the crossing. To allow Ord's men to cross the Big Black, which in 1863 was significantly wider than the modern channel, Union engineers constructed a floating bridge across the river. Finally, Parke's IX Corps, which had been camped north of Vicksburg during the siege behind the exterior line of fortifications, was ordered to move to Birdsong's Ferry.[38]

By the afternoon of July 4, all three Union corps were on the move. Parke's men made it to Young's Crossroads by nightfall, while Steele's Corps, led by Brigadier General James Tuttle's division (which had been posted near Sherman's headquarters at Tribble's plantation) moved quickly to Messinger's Ferry and by the next morning had constructed a bridge across the Big Black. The remainder of the XV Corps left Vicksburg the next day and arrived at Messinger's on the afternoon of July 5. On the southernmost axis of advance, Ord's XIII Corps also left Vicksburg on the morning of July 5, giving the veterans of the XV and XIII Corps at least some time to enjoy the surrender of Vicksburg.[39]

On July 6, all three corps began crossing the river, or at least attempted to. On Ord's front, Brigadier General Peter J. Osterhaus's division marched across the Big Black in the afternoon and was immediately engaged by Confederate cavalry patrols under the command of Colonel William Wirt Adams. At the head of Osterhaus's advance was a small cavalry brigade led by Major Hugh Fullerton. After a spirited fight, the Federals pushed Adams's men back and occupied the village of Edwards and then posted pickets along the roads leading out from town. The rest of Osterhaus's division moved to Amsterdam, west of Edwards, and camped for the night.[40] The middle column, Steele's XV Corps, had to establish a bridgehead on the east bank of the river before advancing. Here, several companies from Colonel William L. McMillan's brigade of Tuttle's division crossed the river and immediately encountered Confederate pickets. Reinforced by the Ninety-third Indiana Infantry, McMillan's troops managed to secure the crest of a ridge overlooking the river crossing by late afternoon. After seizing the high ground, Tuttle's division pushed forward more than three miles and camped for the night on the Bridgeport Road. The remainder of Steele's division crossed without incident and camped behind Tuttle's division.[41]

While the southern and middle columns experienced only minor difficulty in crossing the river on schedule, Parke's IX Corps had a decidedly different experience. With William Sooy Smith's division in the lead, the IX Corps arrived at Birdsong's Ferry early on the morning of July 5. As with the other crossings, Smith was expected to brush aside any Confederate resistance on the opposite bank and establish a bridgehead. The Confederate defenders posted on the east side of the river were led by Brigadier General John Wilkins Whitfield, a rather dour-looking native of Franklin, Tennessee, and a Mexican War veteran. When the war broke out, Whitfield became colonel of the Fourth Texas Cavalry and was promoted to brigadier general on May 9, 1863.[42] Although he was sent to join Johnston in Mississippi, Johnston was apparently no fan of Whitfield, and neither was "Red" Jackson, Whitfield's new division commander. Still, "Old Whit" was popular enough with the men of the Texas brigade and ably carried out his assignment to contest the Big Black crossings. On July 5, Whitfield's cavalrymen were hidden in the underbrush on the opposite side of the river. According to a soldier in the Third Texas Cavalry, the position "was one eminently adapted to a stubborn defense, and commanded an open field through which the enemy must pass."[43] When the lead regiments of Sooy Smith's division appeared, Whitfield's men peppered them with small arms fire. In response, two Illinois regiments from Colonel Stephen Hicks's brigade rushed down to the crossing and dug in near the river bank, which was steeper here than at the other crossing sites. In addition, the water level in the river had risen, making a crossing more difficult even without the Confederate rifle fire. Unable to make any headway against the veteran Texans, Smith sent Colonel William Sanford's brigade south to Jones's Ford, hoping to make a crossing there. Slipping into the muddy water, men from the Sixth Iowa and Forty-eighth Indiana found the river too high and the current too strong to cross. Another brigade, under Colonel Joseph Cockerill, arrived and tried to cross the river a half mile above Birdsong's Ferry. Again, the river was too swift. Stymied by the current and bottlenecked by the pesky fire of Whitfield's

Texans, Parke's corps spent the night on the west side of the Big Black.[44] All the while, Johnston's "Army of Relief" marched east toward Jackson, a movement described by a soldier in the Sixteenth Louisiana Infantry as "a hard and very hot march."[45] Though difficult on the men, the delay afforded by Whitfield's defense of the river crossing allowed Johnston some much needed breathing room ahead of Sherman's juggernaut.

On the morning of July 6, a patrol sent by Sooy Smith discovered an old ferryboat that had been sunk by the Confederates. By mid-afternoon, the boat had been raised and put into service by Smith's men to cross the river under fire. Once Smith managed to get some men across the river, Whitfield's Texans finally pulled back. Work immediately began on construction of a floating bridge, but it was not until mid-day on July 7 that significant numbers of the IX Corps were able to cross the Big Black.[46] The bridge, constructed of logs, now further upset the timetable. Late in the day, Captain George Durrell's Pennsylvania Battery was en route across the river when the bridge collapsed, sending a caisson, two battery horses and one man into the swirling waters. Although the driver managed to grab hold of a log before being rescued, the horses weren't as lucky. According to Private Charles Cuffel, the battery's historian, "The horses struggled in the deep water, their heads now and then coming to the surface in vain efforts to extricate themselves from the heavy harness which held them fast." In a humane gesture, Durrell ended the horses' suffering with his pistol.[47] After the bridge collapse, the remainder of Parke's artillery had to be rerouted to Messinger's Ferry. The rest of Parke's infantry, however, managed to cross on what was left of the bridge, and then quickly moved eastward. By the night of July 7, Parke's lead elements had arrived at Queen's Hill Church, but they were now significantly behind schedule.[48]

Joseph E. Johnston was at his headquarters near Birdsong's Ferry on July 5 when he learned that the garrison at Vicksburg had surrendered. Understanding that his army would now become the target of Grant's troops, Johnston quickly decided to retreat to Jackson. Early the next morning, the army was ready to march. Three of his divisions, all concentrated near Birdsong's, moved east along the Bridgeport Road. Breckinridge's division, which had been deployed near Edwards, marched on the Jackson Road. To cover his army's retreat, Johnston's cavalry, under the overall command of William H. Jackson, did yeomen's work. Whitfield's Texas cavalrymen covered the main body of the army, while Brigadier General George Cosby's Mississippians guarded the army's flank.[49] Led by French's division, Johnston's infantry made relatively good time, marching more than twenty miles in two days, although the heat and dry conditions took a toll on many of the men. A South Carolinian in French's division remembered the march to Jackson as the "severest ordeal through which the regiment was called to pass" during the war. "The weather was fearfully hot," wrote Captain William H. Edwards of the Seventeenth South Carolina. "The roads were dusty and it was impossible to get water to drink. More than half the men gave out, completely exhausted."[50] Robert Patrick of the Fourth Louisiana echoed his sentiments about the march. "We have had a terrible march to-day," he wrote on July 6. "No water—dust, dust, dust. My God it is awful. The citizens all along the route take the buckets off the well ropes to prevent our getting water—and we are suffering for the want of it." Once Johnston's troops began arriving in Jackson on the eighth, he inspected the earthworks surrounding the city with French, who reported that the line was "miserably located and not half completed."[51] As such, Johnston immediately set his men to work strengthening the earthworks. To add to the fortifications, Johnston ordered a large number of cotton bales to Jackson, estimated at more than four thousand. The addition of so much cotton convinced one soldier in the Forty-seventh Georgia Infantry that Johnston was determined to fight. "I think he is going to make a stand here," wrote John Flood. "He is going to fight the Yanks as old Jackson did the English at New Orleans, behind the cotton bags."[52] Slave labor was also used to dig rifle pits and artillery embrasures. During the night, sufficient fortifications were in place to defend the city against an anticipated assault by Sherman's men, as the Federals had done at Vicksburg on May 19 and 22. Included in the line of fortifications, which stretched in an arc around the city, was a series of artillery emplacements, the largest of which was a salient position on the Canton Road north of Jackson known as the Cotton Bale Battery. This earthwork, located near present-day Baptist Hospital, was also known as "Fort Jennie Withers," named for the twenty-year-old daughter of William Withers, a prominent local citizen whose house was located nearby. Inside this large fortification were several Confederate batteries. To the right of this position, Johnston placed a 32-pounder rifled gun positioned above Moody's Branch. Another of these large guns was located along the Clinton Road in a bastion known as "Fort Johnston." This salient position, near the present-day intersection of West Capitol Street and Grand Avenue, covered the approach of the city from the west. More earthworks and battery positions protected the line as it stretched south and then east to the banks of the Pearl River on the southern flank. Along this section of the line, two forts, known as "Fort Breckinridge" and "Fort Lady Gracey," the latter named for the wife of an officer in Cobb's Kentucky Battery, protected the guns of the Washington Artillery and Cobb's battery respectively. All along the line, the trenches and gun emplacements were protected in front by *abatis*, or felled trees, forming a barricade. Finally, in accordance with standard military practice, a number of houses and other buildings in front of the Confederate works were burned to deprive the enemy of sharpshooter positions and to provide a clear field of fire for Johnston's artillery.[53]

After making all these dispositions, Johnston was ready to begin filing his troops into the earthworks. Convinced that Sherman's columns would soon be on the outskirts of the city, Johnston ordered his four division commanders to deploy their men.

Confederate major general William W. Loring. *Mississippi Department of Archives and History*.

Accordingly, on the morning of July 9, men from Loring's, Walker's, French's and Breckinridge's divisions moved into the fortifications. As with any complicated movement, the deployment took several hours. On the northern front was Major General William W. Loring's division, his right flank anchored on the Pearl River. Loring was Johnston's senior commander. A Mexican War veteran, Loring lost his left arm at the Battle of Chapultepec. After being wounded, he reportedly "laid aside a cigar, sat quietly in a chair without opiates to relieve the pain, and allowed the arm to be cut off without a murmur or a groan." While there is little doubt Loring had personal bravery, he had real trouble getting along with his superiors. After a well-publicized spat with Stonewall Jackson in 1862, Loring was sent west. The situation did not improve in Mississippi, though, as he openly despised Pemberton, and his hostility and lack of cooperation showed during the Vicksburg Campaign. At Jackson, Loring commanded three brigades under brigadier generals John Adams, Abraham Buford and Winfield Scott Featherston. The largest of these, Buford's brigade, was a mixture of Alabama, Kentucky, Missouri and

Louisiana troops, while Adams's and Featherston's brigades were largely composed of Mississippi troops.[54]

The next division in line was Walker's, the right flank of which was connected with Loring's near the Canton Road. William Henry Talbot Walker was a West Point graduate and a veteran of both the Second Seminole War and the Mexican War. Known alternatively as "Shot Pouch" and "Old Hell Fire," Walker resigned from the regular army to cast his lot with his native Georgia. Walker's division was composed of Brigadier General Matthew Ector's brigade with four Texas regiments and two Mississippi battalions; Brigadier General John Gregg's brigade of five Tennessee regiments, one Tennessee battalion and one Texas regiment; Brigadier General States Rights Gist's Georgia and South Carolina brigade; and Colonel Claudius Wilson's brigade of five Georgia units and a Louisiana battalion. The four brigades comprising Walker's division faced generally to the northwest and west and connected on the left with the Southern Railroad.[55]

On Walker's left was Major General Samuel Gibbs French's division. French was also a West Point graduate, where he was a classmate of U.S. Grant. A native of New Jersey and a Mexican War veteran, French was wounded at Buena Vista and Monterey. Despite his northern birth, he resigned his commission and moved to Mississippi in 1856 to become a planter. Soon after secession, he was appointed chief of ordnance for his adopted state before entering regular Confederate service. After promotion to major general in August 1862, he was transferred west. At Jackson, he commanded three brigades, the largest of which was led by Samuel Maxey. His was a mixed brigade of Louisiana, Tennessee and Texas troops. Brigadier General Evander McNair, meanwhile, commanded four Arkansas regiments and one North Carolina unit. Rounding out the division was Brigadier General Nathan Evans's brigade of South Carolinians. Generally facing west and stretching south toward the Raymond Road, French's division held the center of the

Confederate major general John C. Breckinridge. *Mississippi Department of Archives and History.*

Confederate defensive line and guarded the anticipated point of advance for Sherman's army. On French's left, and anchoring the southern connection with the Pearl River, was Major General John Breckinridge's division.[56]

Perhaps the most recognizable name among Johnston's division commanders, John Cabell Breckinridge served as the youngest U.S. vice president in history during the Buchanan administration. Born in 1821 in Lexington, Kentucky, Breckinridge served in the state legislature and the U.S. House of Representatives in the 1850s. After two terms in Congress, Breckinridge had had enough of national politics and returned to Kentucky, only to be thrust back into the limelight when he was chosen as vice president in 1856. Then, in 1860, he was nominated for president by the Southern Democrats; the split between Northern and Southern Democrats opened the door for the election of the Republican Party candidate, Abraham Lincoln. Before his term as vice president ended, he was appointed to the U.S. Senate, where he tried in vain to hold the Union together. When Kentucky chose to remain in the Union, Breckinridge fled to Virginia, where he volunteered his service with the Confederate army. Quickly promoted to major general, Breckinridge's service in the Army of Tennessee was marked by repeated clashes with Braxton Bragg, who often maligned the Kentuckians. In May 1863, his division was transferred to Mississippi to serve under Breckinridge's friend Joe Johnston.[57]

At Jackson, Breckinridge's division faced south and was composed of three brigades, including his "Orphans," now under the command of Brigadier General Benjamin Hardin Helm, who was Lincoln's brother-in-law. Helm's brigade also included the Forty-first Alabama Infantry. Next, Brigadier General Marcellus Augustus Stovall, a forty-five-year-old former merchant from Georgia, commanded the "Florida Brigade," composed of the First and Third Florida (Consolidated) and the Fourth Florida, plus one unit each from Georgia and North Carolina. Breckinridge's third brigade, under the command of Brigadier General Daniel W. Adams of Mississippi, was made up of four Louisiana regiments and one Alabama unit. As with the other divisions, Breckinridge had a complement of artillery units. Luckily for the former vice president, the famed Washington Artillery was among those supporting his infantry.[58]

In addition to the infantry and artillery units available, Johnston also had Jackson's cavalry division. After screening the rear of the army as it moved toward Jackson, Whitfield's men crossed the Pearl to watch the army's flanks. Cosby's men, meanwhile, moved to Canton, where they would watch that sector and coordinate with Confederate units in the Yazoo City region. In all,

Johnston commanded an impressive number of veteran troops, with some thirty thousand men available. Once the units were in place, the officers read a message from Johnston. In unusually strong terms, he exhorted his men to defend Mississippi's capital and protect the citizens of the city:

Fellow Soldiers:

An insolent foe, flushed with hope by his recent success at Vicksburg, confronts you, threatening the people, whose homes and liberties you are here to protect, with plunder and conquest. Their guns may even now be heard at intervals as they advance. This enemy it is at once the mission and duty of you brave men to chastise and expel from the soil of Mississippi. The commanding general confidently relies on you to sustain this pledge he makes in advance, and will be with you in your good work until the end. The vice of straggling he begs you to shun, frown on, and, if needs be, check with the most summary of remedies. The telegraph has already announced a glorious victory over the foe, won by your noble comrades of the Virginia Army on Federal soil. May he not with redoubled hope count on you, while defending your own firesides and household gods, to emulate the proud example of your brothers in the east? The country expects in this, the great crisis of its destiny, that every man will do his duty.[59]

Although the supposed victory by Robert E. Lee's Army of Northern Virginia was incorrect—in fact, the opposite was true—Joseph E. Johnston's men were set to defend Jackson against the "insolent foe." The question would be how long their own commander would be willing to hold the city.

CHAPTER 3

"THEY ONE AND ALL PROVED THEMSELVES WORTHY OF EVERY COMMENDATION"

As Joseph E. Johnston delivered his stirring message, Sherman's men were quickly approaching Jackson. The advance, however, had not been as rapid as Sherman might have hoped. The cause for the delay was primarily due to the ever-present Confederate cavalry, who fought a series of skirmishes with the lead elements of the Union advance. The march had also been slowed by the elements, as the oppressive heat and lack of water meant frequent halts. On the evening of July 7, Sherman established his headquarters in Bolton and considered the army's movements for the next day. Having heard nothing from Parke since the crossing of the Big Black, Sherman was in a bit of a quandary and decided to mark time until the whereabouts of Parke's men could be firmly established. Thus, for much of the day on July 8, most of Sherman's men had an opportunity to rest. In the afternoon, once Sherman learned that the IX Corps was safely across the river, he drafted orders to resume the advance at 4:00 p.m. With Fullerton's cavalry again acting as skirmishers, the XIII Corps marched out of Bolton with Osterhaus's division in the lead. As before, the weather was exceedingly hot, with great billowing clouds of dust choking the already exhausted men, resulting in numerous stragglers. With the main road to Jackson packed with soldiers, Sherman ordered the XV Corps to shift to the Bridgeport Road, which ran parallel to the Jackson Road several miles to the north. Their advance would be screened by Colonel Cyrus Bussey's cavalry brigade. Meanwhile, the IX Corps was supposed to move east on yet another road north of the Bridgeport Road, but in reality no such road existed. Thus,

Parke's men were also marching on the Bridgeport Road. Led by William Sooy Smith's division, the vanguard of the IX Corps was soon caught in a traffic jam with Steele's wagon train. Determined not to get further behind schedule, Parke decided to blaze a trail across country, which consisted of gently rolling hills. After "a good deal of labor," Parke's men managed to advance as far the XV Corps. Here, the veterans of the XV Corps had an opportunity to get a good look at their comrades from the east, who appeared entirely different in the type of accoutrements they carried. "They had not yet fallen into Western ways of campaigning," wrote Major David Reed of the Twelfth Iowa Infantry, "but wore complete dress uniforms; carried heavy knapsacks and looked so decidedly worn out and jaded by their march in the dust and mud under a July sun, that our boys felt inclined to guy them and advised them to 'shed' their good clothes, throw away their packs and cease to make mules of themselves." Despite their appearances, however, the IX Corps was in place and ready to resume the advance the next morning.[60]

As all three Union columns converged on the town of Clinton, Jackson's cavalry division continued to fight delaying actions with Bussey's and Fullerton's troopers. "On every foot of ground," recalled a soldier in the Third Texas Cavalry of Whitfield's brigade, the Confederate cavalry fought against overwhelming odds and "force[d] them to pay dearly for every advantage gained." Likewise, Joseph Hunter, a member of Company F, First Mississippi Cavalry, which was a part of Cosby's brigade, recalled that "our cavalry playing around the Federals, first in front and then in rear, had many hard fights and skirmishes in holding them in from foraging the country. We followers of the First Mississippi were on our horses nearly all the time night

"In the van." *From* Battles and Leaders of the Civil War.

and day."[61] On July 8, Fullerton, acting as a screen in front of Osterhaus's division on the Jackson Road, was forced to employ his mountain howitzers on several occasions to clear the way and, when necessary, to dismount his troopers and advance as skirmishers. Osterhaus, observing one of these actions, reported that "the whole of the Sixth Missouri Cavalry were ordered to charge the rebels. Led by their gallant and noble Major [Samuel] Montgomery, they darted down and up the hill, advanced in a splendid line and at a furious gait against the enemy, who did not dare to await the terrible shock, and only offered his back to the galling fire from the Sixth Missouri."[62] After a day of skirmishing, Osterhaus's men halted for the night approximately three miles from Clinton. On the Bridgeport Road, Bussey's cavalry, ranging out in front of the infantry column, also encountered increasing Confederate resistance. On the evening of the eighth, Bussey ran into a strong line of Whitfield's men approximately three miles west of town.

Facing men from the Ninth and Twenty-seventh Texas posted behind a fence rail, Bussey deployed the Third Iowa and two companies of the Fifth Illinois after sending two companies to the right of the road to try to turn the Texans' flank. The column thundered down the road, "charging upon the flying rebs using the pistol and Carbine freely."[63] Forced back, the Texans retreated to yet another position closer to Clinton. As the sun set, Bussey's men ran into yet another line just a mile outside of Clinton, this time composed of Whitfield's entire brigade. After skirmishing with the Federals, Whitfield withdrew. Bussey, however, decided not to pursue because of darkness. On the Jackson Road, Fullerton's cavalry, again screening the advance of the XIII Corps, had not encountered the type of resistance that Bussey had received from Whitfeld's Texans. When within a couple of miles of Clinton, however, Fullerton's troops were brought up short by Clark's Missouri Battery, armed with 10-pounder Parrott rifles. As the Confederate guns had greater range and more punch than Fullerton's mountain howitzers, the cavalrymen called for help from Osterhaus, who sent the Seventh Michigan Light Artillery with its six 3-inch ordnance rifles to the rescue. According to Captain Charles Lanphere, commanding the battery, the Michiganders fired "several rounds with good effect" and Fullerton's men were again able to move forward.[64] With the convergence of two Union corps, Whitfield and Cosby fell back, abandoning Clinton. The delaying action had been hard on the cavalry. Although faced with overwhelming odds and lacking any infantry support, Johnston's troopers had served him well, as the skillful delaying actions provided ample time to improve the earthworks in Jackson and properly arrange for the defense of the city.

As much difficulty as the Confederate cavalry had caused the Federals, the constant skirmishing was nothing compared to the heat and lack of water, which of course affected both armies. In numerous accounts, soldiers blue and gray complained of the extreme summer heat and parched conditions. Augustus Pitt Adamson, a soldier in the Thirtieth Georgia Infantry, wrote that the retreat to Jackson was "extremely warm and the sun shone brilliantly; the roads were dusty, and we had no water, which caused intense suffering and great fatigue."[65] A fellow Confederate from the Third Florida recalled that he "never felt such intense heat; water was scarce; the air was filled with thick clouds of dust and the General stopped but once on the march to rest and then only for a few minutes."[66] With such heat there were plenty of stragglers along the way, and the Thirtieth Georgia was among those selected to pick up any who had fallen out and get them back on the road to Jackson. Those who were unable or unwilling to continue, of course, were likely to be captured by Union patrols. Federal troops on the march suffered perhaps even more than the Confederates. A soldier in the Forty-sixth Indiana listed the temperature on July 5 as 100 degrees, resulting in a march that he pronounced "the most fatiguing and distressing ever made" by his regiment.[67] Henry Tisdale, a soldier in the Thirty-fifth Massachusetts, claimed it was even hotter, writing that it was "very warm, with the thermometer standing at 115." As a result, many of the men in his company fainted from heatstroke.[68] According to George Lee, a quartermaster in Tuttle's division of the XV Corps, the conditions were just as harsh on the battery horses and wagon teams. "Consequently, from want of water, excessive heat, and hard marching, the horses and mules began to die off by dozens," Lee wrote on August 17. "We lost six of our best horses in a day and night. An animal would suddenly begin twitching and rolling its eyes, and in a short time would expire in the greatest agony."[69]

The searing heat and parched conditions were alleviated, at least temporarily, by a violent thunderstorm on Tuesday, July 7. Although typical for summer months in Mississippi, the force and fury of the storm impressed many a soldier. "To night we had a regular old-fashioned Mississippi rainstorm," wrote Lieutenant William H. Bentley of the Seventy-seventh Illinois. "And such a rain! It beggars description. It was a perfect deluge in miniature. During the night we awoke from our slumbers in the [corn] furrows to find high water-mark about half-way up our sides."[70] Charles Haydon, an officer in the Second Michigan Infantry, described the rain as "one of the worst storms I ever saw. The wind blew very hard, the rain fell in perfect torrents drenching one to the skin in a moment's time. The thunder

& lightning I never saw surpassed."[71] Carlos Colby of the Ninety-seventh Illinois saw the storm as an opportunity to get some much-needed water. "The first day's march was the worst in my experience," he wrote.

> *The weather was extremely hot and dry, dust in many places ankle deep, and a very limited supply of water. By 3 P.M. men were falling out of the ranks exhausted, their tongues cleaving to the roof of their mouth, and hardly able to speak. The only visible supply of water was five miles away. When in the west a little cloud appeared, it was anxiously watched as it grew in size—soon a streak of light, with a distant roll of thunder, would it rain, was earnestly asked. Yes, it began to sprinkle, a halt was ordered, those having rubber blankets hastily scooped out a place in the dust, and spread the blanket for a catch basin. By doing so, I caught more than a canteen (three pints) of water.[72]*

On the morning of July 8, the hot Mississippi sun returned with a vengeance, quickly erasing the effects of the storm the night before. One reason for the lack of water, at least as far as the Federals were concerned, was that Johnston's men had polluted the wells, cisterns and ponds along the army's retreat route by driving hogs and cattle in and shooting them, leaving the carcasses in the water. Among those who participated in this odious task was John Kennedy Street, a chaplain with the Ninth Texas Infantry. In a letter to his wife, Street recounted that the Confederates drained the ponds as best they could for their own use and then "threw a dead horse into the balance to keep the yankees, who are in pursuit, from getting any of it."[73] Apparently, they performed their job well, as complaints abounded from the Federals about the animal carcasses in the water. In addition, Charles Cuffel, a private in Durell's Pennsylvania Battery, recalled that residents who had fled the area dumped "tar, turpentine, ashes and other offensive matter" into the cisterns before they departed.[74] Despite this, the Union soldiers, desperate for water, made the best of it and drank the putrid water anyway. "It was not an uncommon sight," recalled David Reed of the Twelfth Iowa Infantry, "to see a soldier step upon the carcass of a mule and dip up water to make his coffee with."[75] The practice of poisoning the ponds and cisterns perhaps made military sense but angered many Union soldiers, who felt it was unjustifiable. According to a soldier in the Thirty-sixth Massachusetts, "such acts only reacted upon themselves, for it enraged the army from the commanding general down to the private soldier, and they would have saved themselves the pillage and devastation that marked our line of march, had they adopted the rules of honorable warfare."[76] To help alleviate the problem, Sherman's men were instructed to take as many mules as possible from the surrounding countryside in order to enlarge the search area for drinkable water.

After successfully stalling the Federal advance west of Clinton, Johnston's cavalry withdrew to Jackson. At Clinton, the main road into the capital city merged with the Bridgeport Road. Sherman, fearing another traffic jam, ordered the XIII Corps to remain in place to allow Steele's XV Corps troops to march past. Thus, Ord's men spent much of the day on July 9 camped in the cornfields west of Clinton. Ord's cavalry, under Fullerton, was on the move, however. Fullerton took a circuitous ride to investigate whether there were any connecting roads angling toward the southeast. Pushing as far as the Pearl River, his men returned about sundown to report that there were several country lanes connecting the Jackson Road with the Raymond Road. This information would be used to guide the movement of the army in the next few days.[77]

Meanwhile, the XV Corps tramped forward on the Jackson Road, with Bussey's cavalry in the lead. Aside from a few minor skirmishes, the way was relatively clear. For the IX Corps, however, progress was barred once again by Steele's wagon trains, which clogged the Bridgeport Road. To make better time, Parke again decided to make a cross-country march. With pioneers building several bridges and cutting lanes through the forests, the IX Corps managed by late afternoon to gain the Livingston Road, which ran northwest from Jackson. Sooy Smith's division was still in the lead and made good time once the Livingston Road was reached. In fact, Smith made such good time that his division far outdistanced the other two divisions of the IX Corps, requiring his men to halt approximately four miles northwest of Jackson. At the Lee plantation, Smith's troops fought a sharp skirmish with some Confederate outposts. Fearing that his division would become isolated, he ordered his men to bivouac for the night in line of battle. Parke's other two divisions spent the night of July 9 north of Clinton.[78]

Steele's XV Corps was also well in advance of the other columns, and Sherman ordered them to halt within four miles of Jackson to allow the rest of the IX Corps and the XIII Corps to catch up. Thus, portions of Sherman's command were isolated on the night of July 9. A more aggressive Confederate commander might have seized the opportunity to attack, but the night passed without incident. Sherman moved his headquarters to Clinton and began working on orders for the morning's advance, which would finally bring his expeditionary force to the outskirts of Jackson.

Sherman's instructions were as follows: Steele would continue moving forward on the Jackson Road until he made contact with the Confederates, who he anticipated would again be in place near the O.P. Wright farm. Two divisions of the XIII Corps (A.J. Smith's and Osterhaus's) were to move via some of the country lanes located by Fullerton's cavalry to the Raymond Road, at which point they would turn left toward Jackson, approaching the city from the southwest. The other three divisions of the XIII Corps would trail along behind Steele on the Jackson Road, constituting a reserve. On the northern flank, Parke's two divisions that had camped north of Clinton were to march forward and join Sooy Smith's division. To assist Parke, Bussey's cavalry was shifted to the army's left flank.[79]

Commanding the XV Corps was Major General Frederick Steele. *Wilson's Creek National Battlefield.*

Early on the morning of July 10, Major General Francis P. Blair's division led the march of the XV Corps toward Jackson. Without cavalry in his front to act as a screen, Blair posted infantry as skirmishers. Meeting little resistance, his men quickly secured the area where the May 14 battle had taken place. Moving with ease, officers and men alike began to think that perhaps Johnston had already departed Jackson. If so, Steele had been instructed to rush one division into town to secure the bridges and public property. The lack of response from the Confederates ended, however, when Blair's lead elements suddenly drew fire from Confederate artillery. It was a big gun, one of the 32-pounders placed in the earthworks beside the Jackson Road in "Fort Johnston." Following the initial report from the Confederate cannon, at approximately 9:30 a.m., other guns opened up on the Union infantry, who promptly sought cover from the unexpected barrage. Sherman, hearing the unmistakable sound of artillery, rushed forward to investigate. Arriving at the front, he ordered Steele to deploy his corps astride the road, with Blair's division to the left and Tuttle's and Thayer's divisions to the right. The position was near the Deaf and

Dumb Asylum, located about four hundred yards west of the present-day intersection of West Capitol and West Monument Streets. The XV Corps bivouacked here in line of battle, where they continued to receive artillery fire from the Confederate defenders.[80]

While Steele's men deployed along the Jackson Road, the two XIII Corps divisions under Osterhaus and A.J. Smith moved as ordered along a connecting lane to the southeast. After marching several miles, the lead troops of Osterhaus's division turned into what they thought was the Raymond Road. In reality, the Raymond Road was a mile farther on, but neither commander knew this. Instead, they had turned into the Robinson Road. Turning left, the Federals approached Lynch Creek, where there was a small Confederate outpost holding the bridge. Charging ahead, Fullerton's cavalry quickly dispersed the Confederate detachment and secured the bridge, and Osterhaus's men hurriedly crossed over. East of the creek, Fullerton's men suddenly came to a halt when they observed Confederate infantry, part of French's division, moving toward them. Dismounting, Fullerton's troopers peppered the Confederates with carbine fire and with their mountain howitzers, causing the Confederates to waver.

Osterhaus, meanwhile, rushed his infantry up to support the cavalry and occupied the ridge east of Lynch Creek, deploying Colonel Daniel Lindsey's brigade on the left and Colonel James Keigwin's brigade on the right. Positioned between the two was the Seventh Michigan Battery. Here, Osterhaus reported that his skirmishers "advanced gallantly on both sides of [the road], against a heavy fire from a formidable battery defending the road, to within 250 yards of the enemy's works." Seeing the disparity in numbers, the Confederates called off their probe and returned to their earthworks. Their retreat was hastened by the Michigan battery, which rained artillery shells into their ranks.[81]

Union brigadier general Peter J. Osterhaus. *Wilson's Creek National Battlefield.*

Osterhaus, now facing what was clearly a fortified line of Confederate infantry, decided to withdraw his cavalry and sent Fullerton's men to scout farther to the right, still assuming he was on the Raymond Road. As the cavalry withdrew, Osterhaus waved his men forward. Advancing just over a mile to within one thousand yards of the Confederate earthworks, the Federals were hammered by French's artillery, likely the guns of Captain Charles Fenner's Louisiana battery. In response, Osterhaus ordered the First Wisconsin Battery forward, and four of its six 20-pounder Parrott rifles went into action on the south side of the road. One of these guns was knocked out by the accurate fire of the Confederate cannoneers, but the Badgers soon shifted their position and disabled one of the Confederate guns, evening the score.[82]

Andrew J. Smith's division now came up in support of Osterhaus, extending the line to the right. Placing the Seventeenth Ohio Battery to the right of Keigwin's brigade, Smith ordered Colonel Richard Owen's brigade to support the battery and held Colonel William Landrum's brigade in reserve. Smith, however, soon learned from Fullerton that there were more Confederates out on the right flank. As such, he ordered Owen to form two regiments, the Sixtieth and Ninety-seventh Indiana, at right angles to the main line. For the rest of the afternoon, Confederate and Union artillerymen blasted away at each other while Osterhaus and Smith's men hastily dug rifle pits.[83] Much of the fighting in this sector centered on a house and cistern, a struggle that the Federals won after advancing two regiments to wrest control of the cistern, which Colonel Owen deemed "so essential to our pickets." Despite this, two men of the Twenty-third Wisconsin died of sunstroke.[84]

Major General Edward Ord's other three XIII Corps divisions—those of Brigadier Generals Alvin P. Hovey, William Benton and Jacob Lauman—remained in reserve until nightfall, at which time Benton's division was ordered to move to the support of A.J. Smith. Once Benton's men arrived, Smith, who was still concerned about a possible threat to his right flank, placed these reinforcements on the right of the two Indiana units that had been positioned to refuse the main line, facing south. "It was not long in this position when the rebel yell was heard and the line of skirmishers fell rapidly back," recalled Adjutant George Crooke of the Twenty-first Iowa. "Bullets from the heavy timber followed them fast, and immediately afterwards the grey-coats came charging." Occupying a house and garden, the Iowans managed to hold off several more assaults throughout the day. Benton's men bivouacked for the night in this position.[85]

Northwest of Jackson, William Sooy Smith's division waited at the Lee plantation on the morning of the tenth for Brigadier General Thomas Welsh's and Brigadier General Robert B. Potter's divisions of the IX Corps to come up. Once they arrived, Parke advanced all three of his divisions toward Jackson. Marching in line of battle, he formed Welsh's division on Smith's left, while Potter's division was held in reserve. Moving east, Parke's men were supposed to pivot to the right once they reached the Canton Road and then move south toward the city, with Smith on the right and Welsh on the left. The IX Corps began its movement by midafternoon, marching through an immense cornfield and then into open country. Here, a soldier in the Thirty-sixth Massachusetts remembered, "It was a beautiful sight…The sun was about an hour high, and its slanting rays glanced brightly from the muskets and the brass fieldpieces. A gentle breeze stirred the silken folds of the standards, and made them float proudly and defiantly."[86] As the IX Corps approached the railroad line heading north from Jackson, Parke's men ran into some of Johnston's cavalry, who wisely beat a hasty retreat in the face of the oncoming infantry. Once across the railroad, the Federals encountered an unexpected obstacle: a dense hedgerow, too thick to get through in line of battle, forced them to shift to a column formation. Once safely past the thicket, Parke's men finally reached the Canton Road. The change in formation, however, had taken time, and it was nearly dark by the time they reached the road and wheeled to the right. As they moved into position, the ever-present Confederate cavalry continued to skirmish with the Federal infantry.[87]

On the east side of the Canton Road, Welsh's men occupied the Insane Asylum ridge. The Forty-fifth Pennsylvania Infantry raised its flag above the asylum, described by one soldier as "a fine, large building situated in ample and rather tastefully laid out grounds." Happily, none of the patients who remained during the skirmishing were injured, though several bullets reportedly hit the building. One of the patients, according to Allen Albert of the Forty-Fifth Pennsylvania, came to the window and made a speech to the Union troops. "I suppose the poor fellow called it a speech," Albert wrote, "although we could make neither head nor tail to what he said. But he was a glib talker all right, and judging from the way he shook his long fingers at us, he must have been a retired politician!" With nightfall, Welsh's men halted and camped. For security, a strong line of outposts was established in the division's front.[88]

William Sooy Smith's division, meanwhile, had a hard time keeping pace with Welsh's men because of more dense brush between the Canton Road

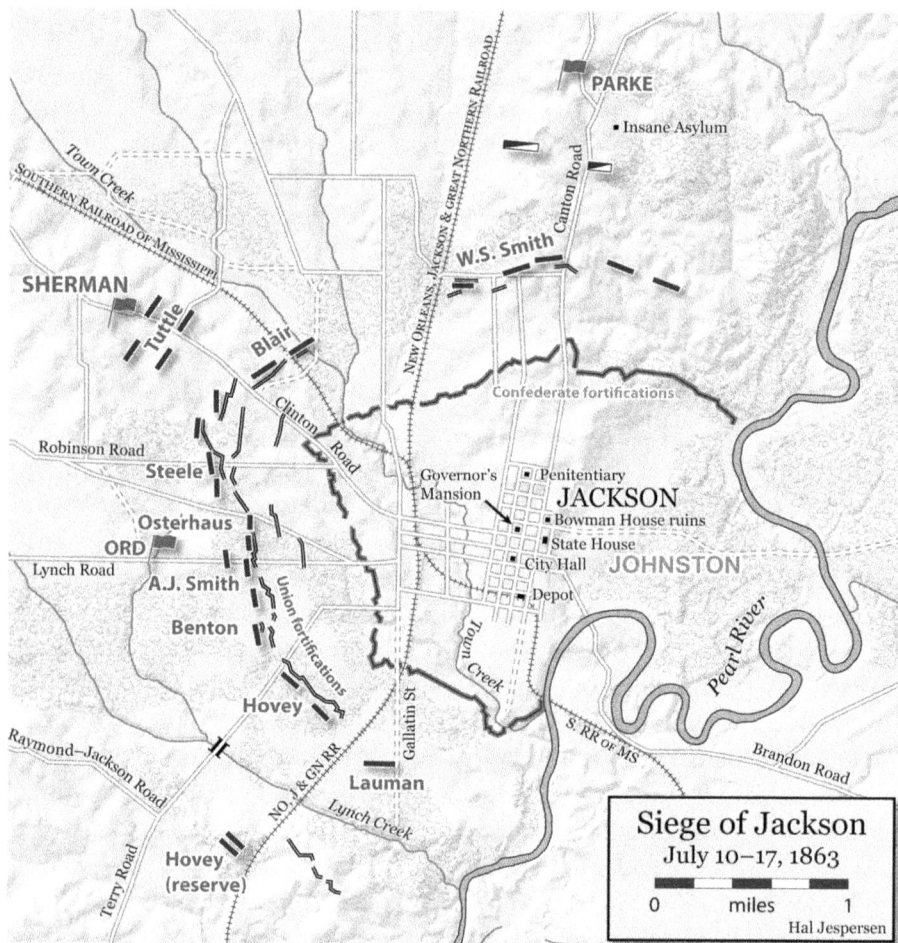

Map of the Siege of Jackson.

and the railroad. As such, Smith and Welsh were not aligned by nightfall, with Smith's division camped on the plantation of former Confederate brigadier general Richard Griffith, who had been mortally wounded the year before in Virginia. To plug the gap between Smith and Welsh, Parke ordered Potter to send two regiments forward from the reserve. As such, the Fiftieth Pennsylvania and the Forty-sixth New York moved forward into the interval between the divisions. The rest of Potter's men camped one half mile north of the Insane Asylum. Out on Parke's left flank was Bussey's cavalry brigade, which patrolled the area near the Pearl River.[89]

Based on the fighting experienced by Osterhaus's troops and the response from Confederate batteries, Sherman was now confident that Johnston intended to defend Jackson. Not desiring to attempt a frontal assault, Sherman opted for a siege and issued orders to his respective corps commanders on the night of the tenth. On all three corps fronts, each commander was instructed to construct artillery positions strengthened with rifle pits and to push the infantry as close as possible toward the Confederate works "without too great a sacrifice of life." Between the flanks of the corps, he ordered picket lines to cover the intervals. On either flank—Parke on the north and Ord on the south—Sherman wanted "frequent and strong detachments" to probe toward the Pearl River in hopes of attacking the railroad bridge or the railroad itself east of the river. Sherman was also mindful of Grant's desire to damage the railroads north and south of Jackson and drafted orders for all the available cavalry to proceed north toward Canton and south toward Brookhaven. Finally, Sherman asked Grant to send another division—Brigadier General John McArthur's—from the Big Black River Bridge to protect his supply train, which might be an inviting target for Confederate cavalry operating in the rear. To protect the bridge, Grant moved two brigades from Vicksburg and Snyder's Bluff. McArthur began moving east and joined Sherman on the afternoon of July 13 after a grueling march.[90]

Union brigadier general Alvin P. Hovey. *Library of Congress.*

The day after receiving orders from Sherman to begin siege operations, troops from all three Union corps began erecting battery positions. On Steele's front, which had been battered by the Confederate's big 32-pounder, the Federals managed to position several batteries on the south side of the Jackson Road, including the four 20-pounder Parrotts of Battery H, First Illinois Light Artillery. This battery was positioned on the grounds of the Deaf and Dumb Asylum within four hundred yards of the Confederate works.[91] Meanwhile, Ord's XIII Corps finally discovered that what they thought was the Raymond Road was in fact the Robinson Road. To fix the situation, Ord ordered Brigadier General William Benton's division, which was at right angles to A.J. Smith's, to form on the left of the Raymond Road. To accomplish this, Benton's men executed a gigantic right wheel, with Brigadier General Michael Lawler's brigade acting as the pivot. With the exception of a firefight in Lawler's front as the division executed its wheel, Benton's troops completed the movement without incident. Unfortunately, the whole division drifted somewhat to the southeast and left a brigade-sized gap between Benton's left and Smith's right. In response, Ord sent word to Smith and Osterhaus to shift to the right and plug the gap in the line. Once all were in position, Ord's XIII Corps divisions dug in, with the exception of Alvin P. Hovey's troops, who were still moving behind the corps toward the Raymond Road.[92] By late afternoon, Hovey's men finally reached the road and deployed with Colonel James R. Slack's brigade on the left and Colonel William Spicely's brigade on the right, stretching between the Raymond Road and the railroad. Moving forward, Hovey's skirmishers encountered Confederate infantry on the north side of Lynch Creek. These men were from the First Arkansas Mounted Rifles and had been waiting in ambush for the Federals to advance. Surprised by the sudden attack, Hovey's skirmishers fell back. To counter the threat, he brought up a section of the Sixteenth Ohio battery, which blasted the Arkansas troops with canister. Once the artillery finished spraying the woods, the Federal infantry resumed its advance. Outnumbered, the Arkansans fell back, and Hovey's men were able to cross the creek, where they camped for the night under a heavy line of pickets. Marching behind Hovey's division was Brigadier General Jacob Lauman's division, which was to deploy on Hovey's right, east of the railroad. Unable to reach their objective before nightfall, Lauman's men bivouacked behind Hovey.[93]

As the sun rose on the morning of July 11, Parke's men, on the northern edge of Jackson, again moved south toward the Confederate lines. With a heavy skirmish line in front, the advancing Federals flushed Confederate pickets from their outposts and back onto the main defensive works. As Union infantry came into view, Confederate artillery began lobbing shells into their ranks from the Cotton Bale Battery. In response, the Federals countered with long-range artillery posted on the Insane Asylum ridge. Welsh's men, continuing their advance, pushed to within a short distance of the Confederate line. The Second Michigan Infantry, commanded by Colonel William Humphrey, pushed too far and got too close. Part of Colonel Daniel Leasure's brigade, the Michiganders were acting as skirmishers for the brigade. Thinking they had been ordered to advance, the Wolverines darted toward the works held by William W. Loring's veteran troops, who were posted on the high ground known as Moody's Hill.[94] According to Captain Charles Haydon of the Second Michigan, the men "crossed the open at a run & without much loss, the men full of fire, yelling like devils." After scattering a Confederate camp at the base of the main defensive line along Moody's Branch, the Second Michigan had almost reached the Confederate works before realizing the rest of the brigade had not followed. In fact, Leasure was about to send support but received word from Parke that the brigade had advanced too far and should be recalled. By that time, it was too late for the Michiganders to stop. Continuing the advance unsupported, they fell back only when it was evident that reinforcements were hurrying to Loring's assistance. Only then did Colonel Humphrey order a withdrawal, taking his wounded with him. Among those was Captain Haydon, who was "whirled around & laid on my back suddenly, very suddenly & in a manner which left no doubt in my mind that I was hit." After regaining consciousness but unable to move, Haydon began to consider his fate:

> *I tried two or three times to rise but finding I could not move I began to reflect on other matters. I now observed that that my hands were laid across my breast & in fact that my whole position was that of the greater part of those killed in battle. I then began to question myself as to whether I were not really dead. I soon discarded this idea but still felt certain that I must die very soon. My whole feeling became one of wonder & curiosity as to the change I believed I was about to experience. I was in no bodily pain & no mental anxiety.*[95]

Captain Haydon, of course, was not killed in the attack. After being rescued by his comrades, he was carried to a hospital and spent months in recovery. After returning to the army, he died of pneumonia in March 1864, never fully recovering from the wound he received at Jackson.[96]

Although they failed to breach the Confederate works, the Second Michigan had done well enough to elicit praise from their brigade commander, who wrote that "they one and all proved themselves worthy of every commendation." Their brief success also convinced Welsh that the line could have been carried had it been properly supported. However, with the repulse, Welsh's division began digging in along the ridgeline approximately one thousand yards north of the main Confederate position. The line occupied by Welsh's troops ran along the high ground near what

An unidentified soldier from the Third Mississippi Infantry, one of the units in Loring's Division at Jackson. *Library of Congress.*

is now Fairview Street. Across the Canton Road, William Sooy Smith's division continued its advance between the road and the railroad until it was in line with Welsh's division. To dissuade Confederate counterattacks, Smith's men also began digging in. Potter's division continued as a reserve, although Colonel Simon G. Griffin's brigade was sent north to begin tearing up the railroad.[97]

To counter the threat from Parke's men on the Confederate right flank, Benjamin Hardin Helm's brigade of Breckinridge's division was ordered to move from the extreme left flank to the other end of the line to bolster Loring's division. With the repulse of the Second Michigan's attack, Helm's brigade was moved a short distance to the west to the rear of the Withers's house and "Fort Jennie Withers." Here, the Ninth Kentucky Infantry was unexpectedly employed in an odd bit of household chores: moving furniture. According to John S. Jackman, the Withers house was located just behind the front lines and was thus exposed to Union artillery fire. To try to preserve the family's possessions, the Kentuckians helped old "Colonel" Withers, who volunteered to shoulder a musket and help man the earthworks despite being just shy of seventy years old, move the furniture out of the house into the back yard. Jackman recalled that just after the furniture had been moved out, a rain cloud threatened to ruin it all, so the Kentuckians began moving it back into the house. "He got all in at a back door save a large mahogany

William Withers's memorial in Greenwood Cemetery. A civilian, Withers was killed near his home on July 12 while shouldering a musket. *Photo by author.*

bedstead which we had to carry to the front door," wrote Jackman, "where the Federal sharpshooters had full view of us, and gave us several rounds, but fortunately no one was hurt." The next day, William Withers was killed in action by an artillery shell and buried in the city cemetery. His tombstone states that he was killed "by a cannon shot whilst aiding in the defence of Jackson, Miss." His remains were later moved to Kentucky.[98]

By sundown, Sherman could be well satisfied that all three of his corps were in position in front of the Confederate entrenchments, with the exception of the far right flank, as Lauman's men had not yet crossed the railroad to the east. Thus far, Sherman's men had escaped any serious bloodshed at the hands of Johnston's veterans, but that would change the next day.

CHAPTER 4

"It Was the Most Sickening Sight
I Ever Saw"

Sunday, July 12, dawned hot and humid. According to a soldier in the Fifty-third Illinois, everything "was as quiet as a Sunday morning could be, with so many men as deadly enemies in a small scope of country." In spite of the constant danger—or perhaps because of it—men in both armies took the opportunity to observe the Sabbath as best they could. In the Twenty-sixth South Carolina, Reverend W.S. Black, a Methodist minister, held a prayer service near the center of the Confederate works. After singing a hymn, the chaplain reported that the men prayed fervently. "The missiles of death, the music of the distant cannon, and the sharp cracking sound of the sharpshooters' guns were in striking contrast with the hallelujahs and praises of that devoted band of Christian soldiers. At such a sight," he opined, "angels might gaze with astonishment and admiration." Unfortunately for many brave men, and especially for those in Colonel Isaac Pugh's Union brigade, the day would not remain peaceful. In fact, this Sunday would be awash in blood before mid-day.[99]

As the third day of the siege began, and with most of the army in position, Sherman decided it was time to begin an artillery bombardment of the city. In orders issued the night before, Sherman instructed his corps commanders to "get as many rifled guns as possible in position" in order to fire on "any groups of the enemy's troops, or in the direction of the town of Jackson, which lies northwest and south of the State-house, plainly visible from all parts of our line." To protect the batteries from Confederate fire, infantry regiments were provided with picks and shovels and set to work at dark to construct fortifications for the artillery. The work was supposed to be completed by daylight on the twelfth, with the cannonade to begin promptly at 7:00 a.m. The bombardment, Sherman specified, was not to exceed one hour and would be limited to thirty rounds per gun in order to conserve ammunition.[100]

The planned bombardment began as scheduled. For the next hour, Union artillery crews fired nearly three thousand rounds of shot and shell into the city. The bombardment had little impact on Johnston's army but resulted in setting several buildings ablaze. While Confederate infantry suffered little harm, Union colonel Marcus Spiegel of Ohio was severely wounded when a defective shell from the Seventh Michigan Battery exploded near the colonel. Later that day, Spiegel wrote to his wife that he had been "dangerously wounded in my left leg, by a shell, a large flesh wound, in the groin. Don't be scared by reports," he told her, "I am doing well as I could." As a result of his painful wound, Spiegel was out of action for several months.[101]

Aside from the damage caused to the city's buildings, the most telling effect of the bombardment was on Sherman's stockpile of ammunition. While the army still had sufficient rounds to repel counterattacks by Johnston's men, Sherman no longer felt he had enough ammunition to maintain a sustained bombardment of the city. As such, he requested that Brigadier General John McArthur, who was then at Champion Hill, send a telegraph to Vicksburg for an additional "4,000 rounds of ammunition for 20-pound Parrotts and 10,000 rounds of 6-pounder case shot." He also requested another one million rounds of small arms ammunition. Once the ammunition arrived from Vicksburg, McArthur would then escort the supply train with a brigade of infantry to protect it from Confederate cavalry. Without the additional ammunition, Sherman felt confident he could "make the time pretty lively."[102]

"Our Works Before Jackson, Mississippi, Sketched Before the Evacuation by Captain Achenbach of Ninety-Seventh Illinois Volunteers." *Mississippi Department of Archives and History.*

As soon as the shelling ended, Brigadier General Alvin P. Hovey, commanding one of Ord's XIII Corps divisions, began moving his infantry forward to align his division with Benton's on his left flank. Pushing his men forward on a line between the New Orleans, Jackson and Great Northern Railroad and the Raymond Road, Hovey soon encountered Confederates in his front, and heavy skirmishing ensued. "The skirmishing soon became very sharp," he reported, "and for an hour the conflict was entitled to the name of battle. The enemy burned several houses in our front, and opened upon us with canister, grape, shell and musketry." Advancing on a two-brigade front with three regiments in reserve, Hovey's men slowly drove the Confederates back. The fighting continued for an hour and a half until Federal batteries were in a position to rake the Confederates in their front. On the Raymond Road, a section of Lieutenant C.M. Callahan's Battery A, First Missouri Light Artillery was placed approximately five hundred yards in front of the Confederate earthworks. According to Colonel James R. Slack, who commanded the brigade on that part of the line, Callahan's battery had a "very fatal effect" on the enemy.[103]

While Hovey's division was moving forward, Brigadier General Jacob Lauman's division was moving to his right to complete Sherman's encirclement of Jackson. Jacob Gartner Lauman was fifty years old, making him the oldest division commander in Sherman's expeditionary force. Born in Maryland and raised in Pennsylvania, Lauman settled in Iowa, where he had success in the mercantile business. Despite no particular military training or experience, he was commissioned colonel of the Seventh Iowa Infantry at the beginning of the Civil War. During the 1861 battle of Belmont, Missouri, he showed his natural ability by leading his regiment into a gap in the Confederate line at a crucial moment. The engagement helped raise both the profile of Ulysses S. Grant as a fighting general and established Lauman as one of a number of capable volunteer colonels in the army. Again distinguishing himself at Fort Donelson, Lauman was promoted to brigadier general on March 22, 1862, commanding a brigade in Brigadier General Stephen A. Hurlbut's division at Shiloh. On October 5, however, at the battle of Hatchie Bridge, Lauman was involved in an action that would bear bitter fruit for him at Jackson.[104]

At the battle of Hatchie Bridge, which took place a day after the disastrous Confederate defeat at Corinth, Lauman commanded a four-regiment brigade. Hurlbut's troops were there in hopes of cutting off and destroying the remnants of Confederate major general Earl Van Dorn's retreating Army of Mississippi. After some initial success, Hurlbut's superior, Edward

O.C. Ord, arrived on the field. Ord, without knowing the terrain in his front, sent two brigades across the bridge in pursuit of the retreating Confederates. Because of a bend in the river, however, the Union regiments did not have sufficient room to deploy once across the bridge. The Confederates, who held the high ground beyond, took full advantage of Ord's blunder, pouring "a murderous and continuous fire" into the ranks of the Union lines. The result was both predictable and disastrous. Despite mounting losses, Ord ordered Lauman, who was in reserve, to send two of his regiments across the bridge and into the confused mass. The result was the same. At this point in the battle, Ord was wounded by a piece of canister and relinquished command to Brigadier General Hurlbut, who sought to end the slaughter. Unfortunately, Lauman misunderstood Hurlbut's orders to pull back and instead sent two more regiments into action before the bloodletting finally ended. While Hurlbut ultimately managed to flank the Confederate position, the damage had been done. All told, the Union suffered more than 550 casualties that day, including men from the Forty-first Illinois Volunteer Infantry, commanded by a fifty-seven-year-old colonel named Isaac Pugh.[105]

A Kentuckian by birth, Pugh was eight years older than his brigade commander, Jacob Lauman. Unlike Lauman, Pugh had served in the army prior to the Civil War; in fact, he was a veteran of both the Black Hawk War, where he served for just thirty-five days and "came out of the war with a bullet hole in his hat brim and a captain's commission," and the Mexican War, where his regiment was credited with capturing $25,000 in silver and Santa Ana's cork leg at Cerro Gordo. In the Civil War, Pugh enlisted in the Eighth Illinois as a captain and then became colonel of the Forty-first Illinois Infantry. At Shiloh, he assumed command of the brigade when the brigade commander was severely wounded. After the battle, however, Lauman was given command of the brigade and Pugh returned to regimental command, a position he held throughout the Siege of Corinth and at Hatchie Bridge. At Vicksburg, Pugh again advanced to brigade command when Lauman was elevated to division command.[106]

During the Siege of Vicksburg, Major General John A. McClernand commanded the XIII Corps on the besieging army's left flank. In June, however, McClernand ran afoul of Grant by publishing an account of the May 22 assault in which McClernand indicated that the assault was unsuccessful because his corps was not properly supported. As neither Grant nor his other two corps commanders, Sherman and McPherson, liked McClernand anyway, this was the perfect opportunity to send the political (and non–West Point) general packing. Promoted in his place, no doubt to the chagrin of Jacob Lauman, was Ord, who had just recovered from his wounds at Hatchie Bridge. Although physical wounds had healed, there was still bad blood between Lauman and Ord over the Hatchie Bridge affair. The continuing conflict between these two men would manifest itself in blood on the morning of July 12 at Jackson.

On the afternoon of July 11, Ord instructed Lauman to "make a reconnaissance, and, if it is necessary to form a line and attack to drive the force in front, do so, so as to keep your connection with General Hovey, who is the connection with the main corps." Because they could not get into position in time before dark, however, Lauman's men camped for the night behind Hovey's division. At dawn on the twelfth, Lauman began moving his division to the right in order to comply with Ord's directive. Crossing to the east side of the railroad, Lauman formed his division on the northern slopes of Bailey's Hill, a prominence from which the city of Jackson and the statehouse were clearly visible. Below Bailey's Hill and extending to the north was a stretch of low ground interspersed with patches of woods and cornfields through which Lynch Creek flowed. When within a mile of the main Confederate line, Pugh's brigade deployed in line of battle, with the Twenty-eighth Illinois on the right, followed by the Forty-First Illinois, the Third Iowa and the Fifty-third Illinois, which was aligned on the railroad. In addition, the Thirty-third Wisconsin was sent to the right to reconnoiter toward the Pearl River while Colonel George Bryant's brigade was held in reserve.[107]

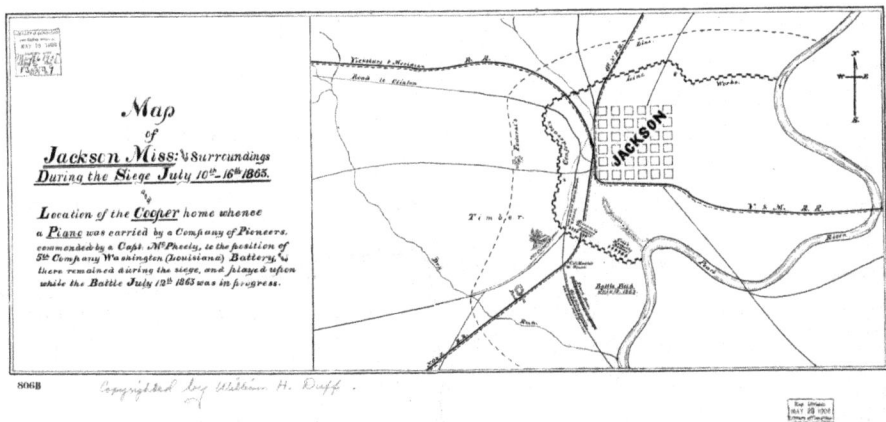

This wartime map of Jackson shows the action on Breckinridge's front on July 12 and the location of the Cooper House. *Library of Congress.*

After aligning his brigade, Pugh waved his men forward. Crossing Lynch Creek, which was lined with timber and dense underbrush, Pugh's brigade moved up to a point opposite Hovey's division on the other side of the railroad and halted. Here, he deployed the Fifth Ohio Independent Battery. Armed with six guns, the Federals lobbed shells into Breckinridge's defensive position astride the railroad. Answering the Ohio battery was the famed Washington Artillery, which had been observing the Federal advance as it moved down from Bailey's Hill. Although the Louisianans had six guns altogether, Captain Cuthbert Slocumb, a thirty-two-year-old native of New Orleans, replied with only two of his four 12-pounder Napoleons, both located to the right of the railroad. The battery also included two James Rifles posted to the left of the railroad.[108]

On either side of the Washington Artillery were the regiments of Brigadier General Daniel Weisiger Adams's brigade, composed largely of Louisiana troops. Dan Adams was the younger brother of Confederate colonel William Wirt Adams. At a young age, he had moved with his family to Natchez. After attending the University of Virginia, he returned to Mississippi to practice law. In 1843, he shot and killed Dr. James Hagan, editor of the *Vicksburg Sentinel* newspaper, whom Adams had accused of libeling his father. Brought up on murder charges, Adams was acquitted by a jury. Ironically, his older brother, Wirt Adams, was killed in a double murder on May 1, 1888, on the streets of Jackson. Wirt's victim and assassin was John Martin, also a newspaper editor whom Adams felt had libeled him. After serving in the Mississippi legislature, Daniel Adams moved to New Orleans to practice law. With the onset of the Civil War, he was appointed lieutenant colonel of the First Louisiana Regular Infantry and steadily rose in rank and reputation. Wounded three times during the war, including a serious wound at Shiloh that resulted in the loss of his right eye, Adams had just returned to duty in June 1863, after recovering from a wound at Murfreesboro, Tennessee.[109]

During the Siege of Jackson, Adams's brigade was composed of the Thirty-second Alabama, Thirteenth and Twentieth Louisiana (Consolidated), Sixteenth and Twenty-fifth Louisiana (Consolidated), the Fourteenth Louisiana Sharpshooter Battalion and the Nineteenth Louisiana, the latter commanded by Colonel Wesley P. Winans. Winans was the only son of the prominent Mississippi Methodist circuit rider William Winans, who before the war had been an outspoken Whig and an advocate for the American Colonization Society, earning vilification by his political adversaries as "an Abolitionist, a free-Soiler, an ambitious aspirant, derelict to the Bible and guilty of nameless but gross immoralities." In 1855, Winans had been mortified to learn that his only son had become a Democrat and had aligned himself with anti-Whig forces in Louisiana. Although the venerable preacher died in 1857, he would likely have been equally distressed to know that his son now led a Confederate regiment in the Siege of Jackson, especially considering there would be bloody work ahead on a Sabbath morning. Four months later, Colonel Winans would be killed in action at Missionary Ridge, leaving no male heirs in the Winans family.[110]

After a brief exchange of fire between the two guns of the Washington Artillery and the Fifth Ohio Independent Battery, Pugh's men moved forward to the edge of a cornfield, where they again halted. In front of them (near the intersection of Gallatin Street and Old Highway 80) the corn had been cut down, and on the opposite side of the field were obstacles of felled trees, creating an *abatis*. Herbert E. Ranstead, a private in Company D, Fifty-third Illinois, remembered the difficulties of the terrain. "This was an awful place to charge across," he wrote. "It was a level piece of ground with a small stream running through it, and the timber had all been cut down and felled toward us and the limbs all sharpened and wire stretched across, and then there were lines of stakes set close together with the ends sharpened and wire on them, and taken it all together it was not a very desirable place to take a Sunday morning ramble under a heavy fire of small arms and artillery." Pugh was understandably wary. "I did not like the appearance of the field," he wrote, "and I did not intend to advance farther without orders."[111] A concerned Pugh sent a courier to ask Lauman to ride forward and inspect the ground himself. Once he arrived on the scene, Lauman instructed Pugh to resume the advance, despite the fact that Hovey's men on the other side of the railroad had halted and had started digging in, uncovering Pugh's left flank. Marching into the cornfield, Pugh's men immediately began taking casualties from small arms fire. After reaching the opposite side of the cornfield, the brigade struggled through the *abatis*, located just three hundred yards from the Confederate line. Suddenly, the tree line beyond exploded with rifle fire, and many soldiers in blue were struck down. Joining the small arms fire were all six guns of Slocum's battery and the four guns of Captain Robert Cobb's Kentucky battery. The gunners had switched to canister and blasted away at the exposed Federals. Directly in Pugh's front were the determined men of Colonel Winans's Nineteenth Louisiana and the Thirty-second Alabama Infantry.[112]

It was along this section of the Confederate line that an unusual incident occurred, involving, of all things, a piano. Near the works of the Washington Artillery, in front of "Fort Breckinridge," was a mansion known as the

Rescued from the Cooper House, this piano was played during the fighting on July 12 by members of the Washington Artillery. *Mississippi Department of Archives and History.*

Cooper House. Burned by the Confederates in order to provide a field of fire, men from the battery, at the family's request, went into the house and rescued whatever items they could, including carpets, books and furniture. The items removed included a piano, which was hoisted over the parapet and into the earthworks of the Washington Artillery. Before, during and after the attack by Pugh's brigade, some of the more musically inclined members of the battery played and sang around the piano in the trenches, serenading their men and General Adams, whose headquarters had been moved to the rear of the fort. Led by Major Graves, who mounted the parapet "like some grand orchestral leader," the men played and sang familiar tunes like "Lorena," "Dixie" and "You Shan't Have Any of My Peanuts." After the siege, the piano was left behind and captured by Sherman's men, but incredibly, the instrument survived the war. Today, the piano resides in the Confederate Memorial Hall Museum in New Orleans.[113]

Despite the difficulty of the terrain and the exposed position Pugh's men were in, the blue line rushed forward into the maelstrom. Major

George W. Crosley, who commanded the Third Iowa Infantry during the attack, wrote that his men "answered this greeting with a shout, and rushed forward to the assault. We were met by a perfect storm of grape, canister, and musketry."[114] They were an easy target. When William Vaught, an officer in the Washington Artillery, saw the advancing line of Federals, he was excited with the prospect of inflicting maximum casualties on the foe. "When I saw those blue coated devils pressing steadily upon us," Vaught wrote in a letter to his sister, "my head grew very slightly warm and my anger began to rise. My body seemed too small for my pent up evil, and I felt like a demon of destruction."[115] To try to escape the trap they had stumbled into, Pugh's men instinctively shifted left, where they encountered more Confederate fire from Brigadier General Marcellus Stovall's brigade, composed of Georgia, North Carolina and Florida troops, which poured withering volleys into the Federal line, and the casualties quickly mounted. Benton Ellis, a soldier in the Third Florida Infantry, recalled that he "never saw such slaughter as our guns made—they were nearly all killed, captured, or wounded. I never saw so many dead men in all my life." In an attempt to bring more firepower into play, a section of the Fifth Ohio Battery was rushed into the fight, only to be quickly disabled by the accurate fire of Cobb's and Slocum's batteries. In the process, the Ohioans lost nine men killed, wounded and missing, plus all of the battery's horses. Without horses to pull the guns off the field, Union infantrymen braved the storm of shot and shell to haul off the cannon.[116]

Lauman desperately called for reinforcements, including the Fifty-third Indiana and the Fifteenth Ohio artillery of Bryant's brigade. By the time they arrived on the scene, however, Pugh's brigade was completely shattered and many of his men were waving handkerchiefs in an attempt to end the slaughter. General Adams, seeing this, ordered a cease-fire and men from Stovall's brigade sallied forth to collect prisoners. Private Henry Reddick of the First Florida Infantry recalled an unsettling encounter with one of the wounded soldiers on the field. "As we went through the woods we came upon a Yankee soldier with one leg and one arm shot off," he wrote, "but still alive and begging for water, but our canteens were empty and none of us had any to give him. It was hard indeed to see a man suffer so and not be able to relieve him with so much as a drink of water, but such is war." Left on the field were sixty-eight dead and more than three hundred wounded, all cut down in a relatively short span of time. Among the dead was the colonel of the Fifty-third Illinois Infantry, Seth C. Earl. Earl, who hailed from LaSalle County, Illinois, was killed near the Confederate works, pierced with four pieces of canister. His body, along with many others, was buried near the spot where he fell. He was later reinterred to the Vicksburg National Cemetery. Of the officers in Earl's regiment, one lieutenant colonel, four captains and two lieutenants were killed, wounded or captured in the assault.[117] Also wounded in the attack was Colonel Aaron Brown of the Third Iowa, who was described as "a large man with a phlegmatic temperament, and an easy-going disposition." Brown, oddly enough, was a native of Marion County, Mississippi. The son of Quakers, he moved north at an early age. During the assault, he was severely wounded in the leg. After months of recovery, he was finally able to rejoin his regiment in Natchez, but

Colonel Seth C. Earl, Fifty-third Illinois Infantry, was killed in action during Pugh's attack on July 12. *Abraham Lincoln Presidential Library*.

he never fully recovered from his wound.[118] Despite the heavy losses, Colonel Pugh's son, Renaldo Pugh, a quartermaster in the Forty-first Illinois, came out unscathed. "It is the strangest thing to me that I am here, alive and unhurt," he wrote his mother the next day. "The very air was filled with shell, canister, grape, spherical case and every other kind of shot."[119] The Confederates, meanwhile, also suffered some casualties, although nothing on the scale of their Yankee opponents. Hermann Hirsch, a soldier in the Third Florida, recalled that as the Confederate skirmishers were forced back onto the main line, "one of our Companie was struck by a Cannon ball in the hip & his side got badly shattered. He died the next day in the evening. About the same time another of my Company had one of his fingers shot off & another lost one of his arms."[120] In the Thirty-second Alabama, Lieutenant Colonel Henry Maury, who commanded the regiment during the action, was severely wounded by a sharpshooter. In all, though, Breckinridge's division lost just seven men.[121]

In addition to inflicting hundreds of Union casualties, the Confederates captured three regimental flags, an exceptionally large number of battle trophies for such a small engagement. As Stovall's men ventured onto the

Sergeant George Poundstone was mortally wounded and captured during the July 12 assault. *Abraham Lincoln Presidential Library.*

battlefield, they captured the flags of the Forty-first, Twenty-eighth and Fifty-third Illinois. After being forwarded to Johnston's headquarters, the commanding general expressed his thanks to the men of the First and Third Florida, Forty-seventh Georgia and Fourth Florida for sending the "splendid trophies."[122] The captured flags were then paraded around the lines. One of the Union soldiers assigned to protect the regimental colors of the Fifty-third Illinois was a sergeant named George Poundstone. The thirty-four-year-old from Grand Ridge, Illinois, was shot in the thigh by a piece of canister during the assault. Despite his wound, Sergeant Poundstone managed to tear the flag from its staff and stuff the banner in his coat to try to save it from being captured. Also shot through the left eye and heart, Poundstone lay on the battlefield with the flag drenched in his blood until he was captured by the Confederates after the battle and taken behind the lines. Though grievously wounded in the assault, Poundstone somehow managed to survive another eleven days before dying in Vicksburg on July 23. His body was later taken home by his father and brother and buried in the Grand Ridge Cemetery. The banner he so desperately tried to protect is also back home. In 1885, the flag was located at the War Department in Washington and returned to Illinois. Today, the Fifty-third Illinois flag, still bearing Sergeant Poundstone's bloodstains, is a part of the Illinois State Military Museum collection in Springfield.[123]

With the repulse of Pugh's brigade by Breckinridge's men, the Federals melted back into the woods and sought cover in the rear. About an hour after the ill-advised assault, General Ord was informed about the attack by a staff officer who reported that Lauman had sent word to his corps commander that he was "cut all to pieces." Riding immediately to Lauman's division headquarters, Ord found him completely disoriented and seemingly unable to put the remnants of his division in order. Ord wrote in his after-action report:

> *I found the men scattered, except that part which had not been with him, and when I called upon General Lauman to take immediate steps to put the remnant of his command under temporary cover, to call the rolls and gather the stragglers, I found he did not know how to do it, and for fear the enemy might follow up their advantage, and the right flank being too important to trust in such hands, I relieved him, and placed his division under the command of Brig. Gen. A.P. Hovey, who at once placed the cut up part of it in the rear in good position, had the scattered regiments collected, rolls called, and reported casualties.*

With Hovey in command, the remnants of Pugh's brigade fell back to Bailey's Hill, and Bryant's brigade, which had not played much of a role in the attack, was ordered to dig rifle pits and gun emplacements on the slopes of the hill. Pugh's brigade, or what was left of it, was out of action for the remainder of the siege.[124]

Before the assault began, Pugh had about 880 men and officers in the ranks. When the fighting ended a little more than an hour later, the brigade had suffered 465 casualties, a loss in excess of 50 percent. In his official report, submitted eight days later, Pugh made sure to note that he was not responsible for ordering the attack and cited his request for General Lauman to examine the ground before he was ordered to advance. Without elaborating further, Pugh wrote simply, "No troops could have done better. All acted nobly, for which they have my thanks and the thanks of a grateful country."[125] While Pugh withheld his feelings about the attack in his official report, he felt no hesitation in expressing his bitterness to his wife, Elvira. In a letter written to her on July 29, Pugh stated that he was in "no way responsible for the slaughter of the men under my command. I do not pretend to say who is responsible but some body is. I think the conduct of Genls. Lauman & others ought to be investigated. The men feel very bitter toward Lauman & Ord."[126] Pugh's son, Renaldo, was more direct. In a letter written to his mother on July 26, he provided further insight concerning the feelings of the men toward those held responsible:

> *It is a miracle that any of us got off that bloody field alive. It was madness to take one Brigade into such a place and it was not the intention to bring on a fight either. Genl. Lauman has been relieved of his command, was put in arrest and relieved on the field an hour after the fight. So you see there is something wrong somewhere. I will not say where, nor who is to blame, but I know a thing or two. Genl. Lauman made a farewell speech to the Brigade but they did not express any sorrow for his misfortune nor did they cheer him. They felt as though he had driven them into a place he had no business to do; and that he had had their comrades murdered for nothing; for there was nothing gained in our assaults on the rebel stronghold. I say driven, it did not take driving, we obey orders and obeyed his on that fatal Sunday. The Col. would not take the responsibility of ordering his men into such a place. He saw what it was and knew it would be folly, ay, worse than folly, madness, to order a little Brigade into such a slaughter pen—for such it was.*[127]

Relieved of his command by Ord for launching the attack, Jacob Lauman's military career was over. Of course, Lauman had accused Ord of virtually the same thing at Hatchie Bridge nine months earlier, but instead of being censured for his recklessness, Ord was promoted to command of the XIII Corps after the removal of McClernand during the Siege of Vicksburg. Like Lauman, McClernand was a volunteer general while Ord, Grant and Sherman were all West Pointers, and that, according to Lauman's defenders after the war, was the true cause of his dismissal. According to Samuel Howard, who served in Company H, Twenty-eighth Illinois, at the bottom of the "slur cast upon General Lauman" was the "deep-seated jealousy which then everywhere prevailed between the Regular and Volunteer officers. This jealously was almost constantly manifesting itself, and was not by any means confined to Generals Ord and Lauman." In addition, Howard claimed there were several men still living in 1906 who could testify that it was in fact Ord who gave the order to attack and that when Lauman protested, Ord told Lauman that "if he would not make the charge, he [Ord] would get someone else to do it." Only then, Howard argued, did Lauman order Colonel Pugh to advance. While this account is not supported by others, it is somewhat consistent with Ord's impetuosity at Hatchie Bridge. Interestingly, despite being relieved from his command at Jackson and sent home to Iowa for the remainder of the war, Lauman was given a brevet rank of major general in March 1865, for "gallant and meritorious duty during the war."[128]

Regardless of who, if anyone, should have been blamed for the disastrous attack, hundreds of men lay broken and bleeding on the battlefield. Incredibly, two days after the fighting, all of the dead and a few of the wounded still lay on the field unattended. In a letter written on July 13, Renaldo Pugh blamed Sherman for the situation, complaining, "Our dead are unburied and the wounded on the field uncared for. Gen. Sherman will not send a flag of truce. Their cries could be heard all night, praying for help—for water." The Confederates not only had to endure the pitiful cries of the wounded but the terrible smell from the decaying bodies. According to a member of the Washington Artillery, "The stench was so great that it is almost impossible to stay in our works."[129]

Finally, Breckinridge, on the fourteenth, asked Johnston to request a truce so the Confederates might go and bury the dead themselves. "The enemy's dead in front of my position are becoming quite offensive," Breckinridge wrote, "and I cannot have them buried because of their [the Federal] skirmishers firing on my burial parties. They have even fired on my litter-bearers while their wounded were being brought in." Johnston agreed to send a staff officer through the lines under a flag of truce to propose a cessation of hostilities to Sherman. In response, Sherman thanked Johnston for the offer to "bury the dead who fell on the south front day before yesterday" and ordered that all firing cease until 4:00 p.m. Sherman also asked Johnston to allow two or three Union officers to accompany the burial parties in order to "recognize and record their names, or, if you are willing to cause them to be collected at any point, I will have them removed and interred." At 2:00 p.m., Johnston replied that the bodies were in "such a state of decomposition that their removal is impossible," and he expressed regret that the proposal had not been made the day before when it might have still been possible to move the bodies of the dead. For the Confederate soldiers who had to endure the horrors of the battlefield, they no doubt also regretted the delay.[130]

The gruesome task of burying the Union dead was left to the men of Daniel Adams's brigade, which also did the bulk of the fighting. Adams

Spare Cartridges, by Alfred R. Waud. *Library of Congress.*

assigned Colonel Leon Toll Von Zinken to lead the effort. Born in Prussia in 1827, the red-headed Von Zinken commanded the Thirteenth and Twentieth Louisiana Infantry (Consolidated). He was known as a strict disciplinarian and an efficient officer, and to accomplish the work before him, he needed both traits, as less than two hours' time remained before fighting was scheduled to resume.[131] To complicate matters, there were apparently plenty of curiosity seekers roaming about, including a few who sought souvenirs. Among these ghoulish tourists was Captain Cuthbert Slocomb, who picked up a sergeant's diary from the Fifth Ohio Battery, while Benton Ellis of the Third Florida "exchanged my old Enfield for a new one, took a rubber blanket and a fine new hat."[132] The situation was so bad that in a note to Breckinridge's headquarters at 2:14 p.m., Adams complained that "no work is progressing from other commands, but large crowds of idlers, &c. are on the ground."[133] Along other parts of the siege lines, soldiers from both armies took advantage of the truce to wander about and visit with their enemies. J.P. Cannon, a soldier in the Twenty-seventh Alabama in Loring's division, remembered that the halt in the fighting was "a pleasant respite from the exciting times of the five days preceding. Many of us met the boys in blue on 'halfway' ground and held friendly conversation with them while the gruesome work was carried on. At 4:00 p.m. the tap of the drum warned us that 'recess' was over, and we hastened back to the cover of our ditches." Lieutenant Henry Nourse of the Fifty-fifth Illinois also found the respite quite entertaining. "All belligerent feelings were apparently left behind with the stacked muskets," wrote Nourse in a postwar account. "Neither the blood that had been spilled nor thoughts of the morrow, with its myriad dangers, cast any spells upon good fellowship and mirth. Jokers in grey and humorists in blue plied their festive witticisms, vying with each other to win the ready laugh of the listeners."[134] Likewise, Samuel Jones of the Twenty-second Iowa enjoyed meeting some Confederates from McNair's brigade:

> *When the Confederates in front of us learned of it they came over to us, and we had quite a little visit. They first wanted to know if there were any Ohio boys among us, there were none. We told them we were from Iowa. They had not seen any Iowa men before. They said they were from Arkansas. They expressed themselves as if they were not much interested in the war, and wished it would soon be over, and thought it would be much more reasonable if the politicians who brought on the war and are still pushing it forward, were made to do the fighting part, rather than to put them to do the fighting who hardly know what the fighting is about. Thus we conversed*

until we received orders to resume hostilities and in a very few moments we were shooting at each other with intent to kill. The last remark made was for us not to shoot until they got within their rifle pits, a request that was always held sacred on both sides of the line.[135]

During these pleasantries, the grisly work continued for the men of Adams's brigade. With no time to bury the dead in individual graves, the unfortunate victims of Lauman's attack were laid in a shallow area converted into a burial trench. Due to the decomposed state of the corpses, the burial details pushed and pulled the bodies into the burial trench (near the present-day intersection of Rankin and Gallatin) with the aid of long-hooked poles. According to a Confederate artilleryman from another part of the siege lines who came to witness the spectacle, "It was the most sickening sight I ever saw." The remains of Pugh's men were not removed until 1872, when they were reinterred in the Vicksburg National Cemetery.[136]

CHAPTER 5

"A PERFECT STORM OF GRAPE AND CANISTER, SOLID SHOT AND SHELL"

On the same day as Lauman's ill-conceived and bloody assault, the Federals on other fronts pushed their lines a bit closer to the Confederate defenses. Throughout the evening of the eleventh and the morning of the twelfth, Union skirmishers exchanged heavy fire with rebel marksmen, described by Colonel Daniel W. Leasure as "a continuous fire of infantry and artillery," often rising to the level of "a battle." Indeed, Leasure reported that his entire line was exposed to heavy enfilading fire of "solid shot, shell, grape and canister, from heavy guns put into battery during the day and night." This Confederate fire came from Loring's men, who continued to strengthen their works. East of the Canton Road, some of Loring's infantry launched a sortie against the Seventh Rhode Island, and on Brigadier General Samuel Maxey's brigade front, the First Texas Sharpshooter Battalion launched an attack against the Fifty-fourth Indiana and Forty-second Indiana, which had moved forward to within two hundred yards of the Confederate line and occupied the walls of a burned-out house. According to Colonel Daniel Lindsey, "The enemy…made a strong sally to get possession of the ruins of the burned house, but were promptly met by the skirmishers of the Fifty-fourth and Forty-second." The Confederate sortie was repulsed by the Hoosiers.[137]

For the next couple of days, the Siege of Jackson devolved into a war of pickets and company-level engagements. Following the disastrous charge by Lauman's men, Sherman made no plans to assault Johnston's line. Likewise, Johnston was in no position to launch a major assault against the Federals. Despite the lack of major combat initiatives by either side, however, fierce fighting continued. Sharpshooters were especially deadly. Flavel Barber, an officer in the Third Tennessee Infantry, wrote on July 14 that the "sharpshooters [are] still annoying us constantly. A person cannot step out of the trenches without danger. Men are shot every day and every hour. The troops," he concluded, "are becoming dispirited and exhausted." On Loring's front, the men continued to improve the fortifications. J.M. Armstrong, an officer in the Lookout Battery, wrote to his wife that "we hauled 60 cotton bales last night and put them in our breastworks, 30 in each & 2 guns. In each place digging dirt and setting posts, until we got our works pretty secure." While Armstrong wrote that the Federals did not fire much artillery against their position, the sharpshooters were active. "Constant skirmishing on both sides all day & night," he wrote, "One man was shot through the breast. He did not die but was expected to." On the Federal side, Lieutenant Samuel Jones of the Twenty-second Iowa also recounted just how deadly the sharpshooters were on the front lines. "We are very close to the enemy's rifle pits," he wrote. "We have only the trees to protect us. The zip zip is as frequent as it is familiar. The boys have a way of locating their enemy by putting their hats on the muzzles of their guns, and pushing them a little out from behind the trees, when zip goes a bullet through them. The smoke of his gun locates the enemy, then it is his turn to take care of himself. Thus we are engaged in killing and maiming."[138]

On July 14, Sherman received a supply of ammunition from McArthur's division and ordered at least a partial resumption of shelling. As a result, batteries in Parke's and Ord's corps began firing rounds from rifled guns into the city at five-minute intervals while Steele's batteries alternated between rifled and smoothbore projectiles. From its position adjacent to the Insane Asylum, Captain John Edwards's Third U.S. Artillery Battery fired 137 rounds of shell and case shot toward Jackson. In response, Confederate gunners fired a few rounds from the 32-pounder, as well as the guns from "Fort Jennie Withers," but the rounds landed in front of Edwards's position and ricocheted over the battery. During the action, Edwards reported the loss of just one horse. Like Edwards's battery, the men of Durrell's Pennsylvania battery used the cupola of the Mississippi state capitol as a directional marker. The purpose of this artillery fire was to induce Johnston to send additional sorties out, but Johnston did not take the bait, choosing to respond only with counterbattery fire. At least one round hit the Insane Asylum building, "creating the widest confusion and terror among the inmates." Luckily, none of the patients was injured on that occasion.[139]

This earthwork, located on the campus of the University of Mississippi Medical Center, was used during the siege by Edward's battery of the Third U.S. Artillery. *Photo by author.*

Besides the exchange of artillery fire on the fourteenth, a much more significant event took place outside of Jackson's siege lines. Johnston learned from some of his scouts that a supply train was en route to Sherman. Of course, this was the heavy artillery ammunition that Sherman had requested. To try and intercept the supply train, Johnston called on William H. Jackson to use his cavalry to capture or destroy the wagons. After consulting with Johnston at his headquarters, Jackson began assembling Whitfield's Texas brigade, which was camped on the east side of the Pearl River. Moving north, Whitfield's men crossed the river on a pontoon bridge near Madisonville on the night of the fourteenth. Joined the next morning by two regiments from Cosby's brigade, the whole force moved west to get around Sherman's flank. This raid could have had dire consequences for Sherman had it not been for a man who "escaped" from the ranks of Jackson's cavalry division and suddenly appeared at Parke's headquarters, where he gave a detailed report to Parke the next morning.[140]

This "deserter" was identified as A. Leroy Carter, who claimed to be a soldier in the Third Iowa Infantry. Indeed, there was a soldier by that name who enlisted with the regiment in 1861. According to the unit's roster, he had been severely wounded in September 1861 and then reenlisted in December 1863, with no additional details of his service in between. According to the story Carter related to Parke, he had been captured in early January 1863 and had since been serving as a either a blacksmith or farrier for Jackson's cavalry division. After providing an outline of the planned raid, Carter gave detailed troop strengths for each of Jackson's cavalry regiments, which was quite an accomplishment for a prisoner serving in a support role. The same day that Carter suddenly appeared at Parke's headquarters, Confederate captain Samuel Henderson, who commanded an independent company of scouts, reported to Johnston that two of his men had been ambushed on the morning of the fifteenth near Calhoun Station. Henderson stated that one of his scouts—also by the name of Carter—had been captured. Supposing the Federals had shot his horse, Henderson considered his capture was "a very serious loss to my command," as he was "one of the best men I ever knew." His purpose in writing Johnston was to report that another Federal force was moving up toward Yazoo City, but his note about the capture of the scout named Carter is interesting, to say the least. Whether just an amazing coincidence, or whether Carter was an incredibly observant prisoner, a trusted scout or a Union spy may never be known. The fact is, however, a man named Carter provided incredibly detailed and important information at just the right time to Sherman, who immediately relayed the information to Grant.[141] In response, Colonel Alexander Chambers's brigade at Champion Hill was ordered to accompany the supply train and Major General Francis J. Herron's division, the force Henderson reported to be at Yazoo City, was ordered to move east toward Canton to protect Sherman's left flank. Meanwhile, Sherman took measures to reinforce the Seventy-eighth Ohio Infantry at Clinton, where the Federals used the mostly abandoned buildings at Mississippi College as a hospital. To bolster the Clinton garrison, Sherman ordered Brigadier General Charles Matthies's brigade of MacArthur's division to march to the Ohioans' aid. That night, Jackson's cavalrymen, unaware that their plans had been revealed, camped north of Clinton. The next morning, the gray-clad horsemen moved to the attack.

At daybreak on the sixteenth, Jackson's cavalry descended on Clinton by way of the Livingston and Brownsville Roads. Advancing in two columns, the Confederates were surprised to find that the pickets of the Seventy-eighth Ohio were ready and waiting. After the Union outposts opened fire, Jackson deployed his division and forced the Union skirmishers

The Supply Train, by Edwin Forbes. *Library of Congress.*

back. Matthies's brigade then came to the support of the Seventy-eighth Ohio, and after an hour's firefight, the Confederates, facing a brigade of Union infantry, withdrew toward Brownsville, northwest of Clinton.[142] The same day, Jackson sent a smaller force to Bolton, where they captured eight wagons loaded with rifles, pistols and "plenty of eatables including coffee," a meal promptly devoured by the hungry men of the Third and Ninth Texas Cavalry. In addition, eighty-three unlucky Federals were taken prisoner. The nearby ammunition train, however, was too heavily guarded by Chambers's brigade and eluded capture. Unable to complete his mission of halting the supply train, Jackson withdrew to the vicinity of Vernon. Sherman's ammunition train, now safe from the threat of Confederate cavalry, lumbered on toward Jackson and arrived on the night of the sixteenth. The failure of Johnston's cavalry to stop the progress of the supply wagons, thanks in part to the elusive Leroy Carter, was of critical importance. As a result, Joseph E. Johnston immediately began developing plans to abandon the city of Jackson.[143]

While all this occurred north and west of town, siege operations continued without much fanfare, with the exception of a brief flurry of activity on the southern end of the Union line. On the fifteenth, a Union patrol from Colonel Cyrus Hall's brigade discovered that a Confederate patrol had crossed the Pearl River and established an outpost in the rear of the XIII Corps. After reporting this information to Alvin P. Hovey, Hall and Colonel George Bryant assembled a force of six regiments and began moving toward the outpost. Sighting this heavy column, the Confederates wisely re-crossed the river.[144] Otherwise, soldiers in both armies spent their time dodging the ever-present sharpshooters. On the morning of the sixteenth, however, Parke launched a heavy reconnaissance to test the strength of the Confederate lines in front of the IX Corps. For this, he ordered William Sooy Smith's and Robert Potter's divisions to press toward the Confederate works with a strong line of skirmishers. The movement was slated to begin at 11:00 a.m. with Smith's men advancing west of the Canton Road. Commanding this portion of the reconnaissance was Colonel John M. Corse. Corse had five regiments at his disposal, including the Sixth Iowa and the Ninety-seventh Indiana deployed on the front line as skirmishers. The Hoosiers would advance with their left on the Canton Road and their right on the NOJ&GN Railroad while the Iowans were positioned with their right on the Southern Railroad. Corse's other three regiments—the Fortieth and Forty-eighth Illinois and Forty-sixth Ohio—were held in reserve. East of the Canton Road, Potter assigned Brigadier General Edward Ferrero. Compared to Corse's command, Ferrero's force was small, composed of just six hundred men.[145]

At the appointed time, Edwards's battery fired two rounds to signal the advance, and Corse's and Ferrero's men moved out. Ferrero's troops, composed of men from the Forty-sixth New York Infantry, a mostly German regiment, advanced across open ground toward the Confederate line. The regiment's advance immediately drew fire from the guns of the Cotton Bale Battery. Lieutenant Colonel George Travers, who commanded the regiment during the advance, reported that the New Yorkers had been ordered to advance slowly in order to "feel the enemy's position, and, in case he should be found still in his rifle-pits in force, to fall back." As the regiment advanced, they drove the Confederate outposts on to the main line of rifle pits. After an hour, though, Travers felt that he had accomplished his mission and recalled his troops. Killed in action during the advance was Heinrich Oppermann, a forty-year-old private from New York City. Unfortunately, when the New Yorkers pulled back, the left flank of the Ninety-seventh Indiana was left dangerously exposed.[146]

With its left flank on the Canton Road, the Ninety-seventh Indiana, commanded by Colonel Robert F. Catterson, advanced simultaneously with the Forty-sixth New York and the Sixth Iowa on the regiment's right. Corse reported that the regiment moved forward "briskly," all the while exposed to "a galling fire of musketry from the parapet of the enemy's works" as well as Confederate artillery.[147] In addition, the Hoosiers drew fire from sharpshooters of the Twentieth Mississippi Infantry, who were hidden in a patch of woods to the left of Catterson's line. Despite the annoyance of the Mississippi sharpshooters, the Ninety-seventh Indiana pushed forward to within two hundred yards of the main Confederate line, all the while enduring "a perfect storm of grape and canister, solid shot, and shell."[148] Unfortunately, the regiment advanced unsupported, as the Fortieth Illinois had not yet arrived when the signal to advance was given. Caught in the open and seeing that any further advance would "be death to every man," Catterson ordered his regiment to halt, taking advantage of a small ravine while he waited for reinforcements. Although this ravine provided some shelter, the position was still exposed to fire from Loring's division. The experience was a trying one. Andrew Bush complained to his wife that "they was eleven pieces of canon right in front of us and two that cross fired on us they threw shells and grape Shot at us from ten o'clock in the morning until five in the evening." At last, the Fortieth Illinois moved down the slope to support the Hoosiers, but due to the storm of iron and lead, the Illinois troops also took shelter in the ravine, to the right and rear of the Ninety-seventh Indiana. Here, according to Sergeant E.J. Hart of Company E, the regiment lay for four hours with "shot and shell flying thick and fast" overhead.[149]

To the right of the Ninety-seventh Indiana and Fortieth Illinois, the Sixth Iowa also advanced into the maelstrom. "Clearing the timber," wrote Colonel Corse, the regiment "rushed out into the open fields, across the railroad, over the fence, up a gentle slope, across the crest, [and] down into the enemy's line, where two field batteries of four guns each, fronting west, opened a terrific cannonading." The advance of the Sixth Iowa caught some of the Confederate outposts in the open and drove them back on the main line, but now the Iowans were completely exposed. Henry Wright recalled that "the batteries of the enemy opened terrific fire with canister shot and shell, whereupon the bugle sounded the 'lie down.'" It was Corse who ordered the regiment down, as a Confederate battery six hundred yards to the right was "throwing its whirlwind of grape and canister about us until the corn fell as if before an invisible reaper." Looking around, he did not like the look of things. On his right, front and left, the Confederates had both field guns and heavy artillery aimed at his men, all supported by lines of Confederate infantry. "To pass through the batteries, cross the regiments in our front, ascend the hill, and get inside their main works," Corse determined, "was more than I could accomplish with the slender but gallant line lying to my left and right." As such, he ordered the regiment to rise and retreat. According to Wright, John R. Simpson, the bugler, blew the call to "rise" and "retreat" in quick succession and "in notes which were trembling but clear and distinct." In retreating over the same ground, the Iowans were again exposed to the converging fire of the Confederate batteries. When the Sixth Iowa retreated, the Fortieth Illinois also fell back. Miraculously, the regiment suffered only one man killed and five wounded during this action. With both his right

Although this image is from the Atlanta Campaign, these soldiers are employing the same methods used at Jackson to dismantle the railroads. *Library of Congress*.

and left flank now exposed, Colonel Catterson finally ordered the Ninety-seventh Indiana to retreat, although only the right half of his line was able to withdraw under fire. The left portion of the regiment remained in close proximity to the main Confederate works. Since the purpose of the forced reconnaissance was to establish that Johnston's men were still in place, Parke had accomplished what he set out to do.[150]

At the outset of the expedition to Jackson, Grant expressed his desire that Sherman cause as much damage as possible to the railroad network. As early as the eleventh, Sherman was already at work ensuring that Grant's directive was met. To accomplish this mission, work crews from various regiments began tearing up the tracks north of Jackson in Parke's sector. In addition, Sherman ordered Bussey's cavalry to march north toward Canton to rip up the rails and destroy whatever supplies he found there. Located approximately twenty-five miles from Jackson, Canton was the Madison County seat and had been thriving since the arrival of the New Orleans, Jackson and Great Northern Railroad in 1856. From there, the line continued northward as the Mississippi Central Railroad. In addition to the usual railroad facilities, Canton was the home of the Dixie Works, which produced an assortment of items for the Confederate government, including wagons, ambulances, light artillery carriages and perhaps even swords and bayonets. The presence of the Dixie Works, plus the engine houses and other buildings associated with the railroad, made Canton an inviting target for Federal troops.[151]

Colonel Cyrus Bussey was a Democratic state senator in Indiana prior to the war. After being elected colonel of the Third Iowa Cavalry in 1861, he was in active service in Arkansas. During the Vicksburg Campaign, the regiment was sent to Snyder's Bluff north of Vicksburg, where it was joined by the Second Wisconsin, Fourth Iowa and the Fifth Illinois Cavalry. Cobbled together as a cavalry brigade, this makeshift force was used to patrol the "Mechanicsburg Corridor" between the Big Black and Yazoo Rivers. On June 26, Sherman ordered Bussey's men to the area to try to discover what the Confederates were up to. Bussey rode north as instructed but managed to avoid any contact with the enemy, reporting rather nonchalantly upon his return that he "saw nothing of interest." Sherman was not pleased with this seemingly lackluster performance, complaining to Grant that "as usual, my cavalry are not bold." Despite his misgivings about the effectiveness of his horsemen, it was Bussey's brigade that was assigned the task of raiding Canton. Unfortunately, Bussey's performance would again disappoint the fiery Sherman.[152]

Late in the afternoon on July 11, Bussey's men left their camp near the Insane Asylum and rode north on the Livingston Road. After turning east toward the railroad, the brigade arrived at Midway about 10:00 p.m. (near modern-day Madison). Here, the men of the Third and Fourth Iowa began dismantling the railroad. After two hours of hard work, the Iowans managed to wreck a half mile of track. Moving north, they halted for the night two miles south of Calhoun Station, which is present-day Gluckstadt. Early the next morning, the brigade rode into Calhoun, where it destroyed two locomotives and twenty-five railroad cars, along with the depot. Continuing north, the Federals were about to cross Bear Creek, just south of Canton, when they were fired on by Confederate cavalry under the command of George Cosby. A native Kentuckian, Cosby was a skilled cavalry officer and a West Point graduate. His brigade was part of Jackson's cavalry division and included the First Mississippi, Fourth Mississippi, Peter Starke's regiment and Wirt Adams's cavalry regiment. Cosby was no stranger to Bussey; in fact, it was Cosby's men Bussey had so "skillfully avoided" in June. Now, after a heavy skirmish, Bussey chose not to bring on an engagement and instead made a circuitous ride through Madison County, finally returning to Jackson on the morning of July 13. Although they had been gone for two days, the expedition had accomplished little, a fact that did not escape the attention of some of Bussey's men. John Preston Mann, an officer in the Fifth Illinois, complained that Bussey's refusal to push his way into Canton meant that he was "not fit to command a troop and should quit." Sherman, of course, was also displeased with the result and immediately decided to send another column toward Canton. This time, however, the column would be reinforced with an infantry brigade that would accompany the cavalry on its journey north.[153]

At the same time that Sherman ordered Bussey's men to Canton, he also directed Ord to send all his available cavalry on an expedition to do damage to the railroad south of Jackson. The XIII Corps cavalry consisted of just fourteen companies from the Second and Third Illinois, Fourth Indiana and Sixth Missouri. In all, the force numbered approximately five hundred men and was commanded by Major Hugh Fullerton. Fullerton's men did not get moving as quickly as Sherman might have hoped, as they were still engaged in patrolling toward the Pearl River on July 10 and 11. They finally moved out at 10:00 p.m. on the eleventh, however, and proceeded to Byram, a small community located about twelve miles south of Jackson. At Byram, Fullerton's men burned a railroad bridge, tore up some tracks and destroyed the depot, water tank and several freight cars. Although they encountered little opposition, the raiders turned back toward Jackson because Fullerton claimed he did not have the tools to do much more damage. "I tore up but little of the track," he wrote, "for the reason that I had nothing in the world to do it with."[154]

Determined to wreak greater havoc on the railroads south of Jackson, Sherman ordered Fullerton to give it another try. This time, Fullerton's task force included a mounted infantry battalion, commanded by Colonel John G. Fonda, a veteran of the Mexican War. Despite receiving orders to move out on the sixteenth, Fullerton's men did not depart until the next morning, when the column finally moved down the railroad to Terry, where they halted for lunch and began tearing up track. After leaving Terry, Fullerton's men passed through Crystal Springs after dark, where his men learned that a train had departed just twenty minutes before their arrival. Camping for the night on a nearby plantation, the raiders were on the road at 8:00 a.m. and moved to Hazlehurst, where they burned the depot and a large supply of lumber. Next, the column moved to Bahala (present-day Beauregard), where they again destroyed the depot and about twenty rail cars. Finally, at noon on the eighteenth, Fullerton's men arrived at Brookhaven. For the first time during the expedition, the Federals encountered Confederate opposition, although it was minimal. After light skirmishing, they managed to capture forty-five prisoners, including Major George McKnight, a Louisianan and assistant adjutant general for General William W. Loring. After being taken prisoner, McKnight was sent to the Union prison camp at Johnson's Island in Ohio. While there, he made the most of his time, writing poetry and putting on theatrical performances for his fellow prisoners, which "enlivened the dreary camp and prison life of the Southern soldier." After the war, several of his poems were published in the *Confederate Veteran* magazine under his pseudonym, Asa Hartz.[155]

In addition to taking prisoners, Fullerton's men found and destroyed several locomotives and freight cars and captured a large shipment of Confederate mail. It was the mail shipment that, almost a year later, caused a minor international incident. In May 1864, Lord Richard Lyons, the British Envoy to the United States government, wrote a letter to U.S. secretary of state William H. Seward indicating that letters and diplomatic dispatches from Her Majesty's Consul in Galveston, Texas, had been opened and destroyed during a Union raid the previous summer. "Not only were the seals of this packet broken," wrote Lord Lyons, but the dispatches themselves "were torn and thrown into the streets." Lyons, who was well acquainted with Seward, asked that the matter be investigated. Three months later, Seward finally responded to the request with an enclosed report from Lieutenant Benjamin F. Garrett of Company K, Second Illinois Cavalry. In his report, Garrett explained that he was ordered by Fullerton to examine the mail "and see if any knowledge of importance could be gained therefrom." Garrett stated, however, that he did not have time to complete a thorough examination but that he found "no dispatches in said mail from Lord Lyons, or any foreign dispatches or papers of any kind whatever," and that he destroyed no mail whatsoever. "If said mail, or any part thereof, was destroyed," Garrett stated, "it was done by irresponsible and unauthorized parties." Apparently, Seward's response satisfied Lord Lyons, as no further inquiry was forthcoming.[156]

Following the destruction of property at Brookhaven, Fullerton's men returned to Jackson by way of Gallatin and Crystal Springs with their prisoners in tow. The loss of Confederate supplies at Brookhaven might have been much worse had it not been for the alertness of Major Robert S. Carter of the Seventh Mississippi Infantry, who commanded the post at Brookhaven. "I evacuated the place several days before their arrival," wrote Carter, "securing all the stores in my possession save 300 bushels of corn." In his report, Carter said Fullerton's raiders burned "300 hogsheads of sugar, destroyed the post-office, and burned 2 engines and all the rolling stock" before heading back north. Fullerton's men arrived in Jackson on the morning of the twentieth after riding 120 miles in four days. During the raid, the brigade lost just one man, Major John L. Campbell of the Third Illinois Cavalry, who was mortally wounded.[157]

The same day that Fullerton was supposed to move south (on July 16), Bussey's cavalry, now reinforced with an infantry brigade under Colonel Charles R. Woods and a battery of Missouri artillery, again moved toward Canton. A native of Ohio, Charles Woods graduated from West Point the same year as George Cosby, after which he served in the regular army at various posts out West until the outbreak of the Civil War. Curiously, his first service was aboard an oceangoing vessel. In 1861, Woods commanded the troops on board the *Star of the West*, which had been sent to relieve Fort Sumter in Charleston Harbor. Although the relief effort was unsuccessful because the ship was fired on and had to turn back, the encounter is hailed as one of the first shots of the Civil War. Ironically, the *Star of the West* later fell into Confederate hands and was eventually scuttled in the river channel near Greenwood, Mississippi. As colonel of the Seventy-sixth Ohio Infantry, Woods had mostly fought in the Western Theater. By the late spring of 1862, he was given command of a brigade, and during the Vicksburg Campaign

Union colonel Charles R. Woods, whose brigade was known as the "German Light Brigade" for the large number of German immigrants in its ranks. *Library of Congress.*

was one of Sherman's XV Corps brigadiers. For the Canton expedition, Woods's brigade consisted of two Iowa regiments, one Ohio unit and three regiments from Missouri. The Missouri units—the Third, Twelfth and Seventeenth—were composed largely of German immigrants.[158] Among these troops was a soldier named Charles Junghaus, who was shot in the head and killed at Resaca, Georgia, on May 17, 1864. In 1866, as remains of Union soldiers were being reinterred to the Chattanooga National Cemetery, it was discovered that Charles Junghaus was in fact a woman. She is one of three female soldiers believed to have served with Sherman's army at Jackson.[159]

On the sixteenth, the combined force, numbering approximately two thousand, marched north on the Canton Road toward Grant's Ferry on the Pearl River. After a brief skirmish with Confederate pickets, the Federals burned a supply of lumber and a ferryboat. Before leaving Grant's Ferry, Bussey sent Colonel Edward F. Winslow's Fourth Iowa Cavalry, along with the Fifth Illinois Cavalry, to destroy a pontoon bridge near Madisonville. With his mission completed, Winslow rejoined the main force at Calhoun Station. There, Woods's men were engaged in the destruction of the railroad. By the next morning, they had ripped up one mile of track and burned a bridge. Moving farther north, the Federals suddenly encountered Confederates under the command of William H. "Red" Jackson, who had assembled three cavalry brigades in Canton. In response, Bussey—who was in overall command of the expedition—ordered Woods to deploy two of his regiments on either side of the road. Soon after Woods deployed his infantry, Bussey observed "a large force of the enemy moving to our left to gain our rear." To counter the flanking movement, Bussey sent a portion of the Fifth Illinois Cavalry to the left flank, which arrived in time to temporarily force the Confederates back. Jackson now brought up his own reinforcements and renewed the effort to turn the Federal flank. To counter this new threat,

Bussey sent in the Third and Fourth Iowa Cavalry, and Woods deployed the Twenty-fifth Iowa and Seventy-sixth Ohio Infantry Regiments, which had been guarding the wagon train. "When the Rebels attacked, our troops were rapidly formed into line of battle with skirmishers to the front," wrote Major Charles Dana Miller of the Seventy-sixth Ohio. "We left the road and moved through a thick hedge fence into open fields with a battery that tossed some shells into the Rebel column as it passed." Faced with a formidable line of infantry, cavalry and artillery, the Confederates abandoned the flanking movement. After the crisis had passed, Miller rode up to a small house that had been hit by one of the Union artillery rounds. Entering the house, he found an elderly couple. On inquiring if anyone had been hurt, he discovered that the cannonball had passed completely through the house and over the head of the bedridden old man. Spared was the couple's prized clock, which the old man attributed to it being "a Yankee clock."[160]

While the fight on the left flank was under way, Colonel Woods moved the Twelfth Missouri Infantry and the Second Wisconsin Cavalry forward in an effort to capture the bridge spanning the steep banks of Bear Creek. As the Twelfth Missouri approached the bridge, however, Confederate artillery from Clark's Missouri Battery opened fire with two guns, a rifled 6-pounder and a 12-pounder smoothbore. The Missouri Federals swept forward but were unable to capture the bridge before it was burned by the Confederates and, due to the accurate fire of Clark's battery, were forced to retire. Next, Woods decided to send two regiments to the right to find another crossing. With the Twelfth Missouri and Seventeenth Missouri left to skirmish at long range with the Confederates on the opposite side of creek, the Third Missouri, supported by the Twenty-fifth Iowa, moved through the woods to the east. Finding a section of the creek that was fordable, the two regiments splashed across the creek and engaged with Confederate skirmishers. Realizing his position was now untenable, Jackson retreated toward Canton and then crossed to the east side of the Pearl River, much to the dismay of Canton's citizens, who, according to the local editor, "were anxious to see a trial of strength between the enemy's and Jackson's forces, and were willing to submit to any sacrifices that the fortunes of war might entail upon them." After seizing the north bank of Bear Creek, Woods ordered his men to rebuild the bridge, which they accomplished by nightfall. Woods's men camped for the night on the north side of the creek and entered Canton on the morning of July 17.[161]

Woods's and Bussey's men were now in control of Canton, described by a Missouri soldier as "a beautiful town." The Federals immediately went to work destroying the railroad shops, yards, locomotives and cars. In all, the task force wrecked thirteen machine shops, five locomotives, thirty rail cars, two turntables and a large lumber yard. As for the Dixie Works, Woods reported that the factory had been "effectually destroyed." However, the whole building was not burned, as it would have required the destruction of an entire block of buildings. Two months later, the manufacturer relocated to Macon, Georgia.[162] Aside from the destruction of the railroad shops and the Dixie Works, the Federals captured some amount of Confederate war materiel, including a large stack of unsigned and uncirculated Confederate currency. To the delight of the men in the Seventy-sixth Ohio, the Union soldiers took turns signing the bills themselves and then distributing them to the citizens, who took them as payment for supplies and "didn't know the difference." Unlike other towns, there was almost no damage to any civilian property in Canton, as guards were posted by Bussey to prevent looting. Occupied by Union troops during the Meridian Expedition in 1864, Canton again escaped any significant damage. As a result, modern-day Canton boasts a large number of antebellum structures, including the county courthouse, built in the 1850s.

After completing their work of destruction in Canton, Bussey's men rode back across Bear Creek and camped for the night on the south bank. Meanwhile, Edward Winslow's Iowans were on their way to Way's Bluff, where the railroad crossed the Big Black River north of Canton, with orders to burn the bridge. Returning that night, Winslow reported the destruction of the bridge, plus a mile of trestle work and the depot at Way Station. The next day, July 19, the expedition returned to Jackson. The five-day sojourn had been a success. By the time Bussey's command returned to Jackson on July 20, Joseph E. Johnston had abandoned the city to Sherman's troops and escaped across the Pearl River.[163]

CHAPTER 6

"THE CITY...IS ONE MASS OF CHARRED RUINS"

On the afternoon of July 16, Joseph E. Johnston decided that the time had come to save his army from destruction. He made the decision to evacuate Jackson after his cavalry failed to intercept Sherman's ammunition train and because he had observed additional gun emplacements going up along the Federal siege lines. Both indicated that Sherman would soon begin a heavy bombardment of the city. In light of this, Johnston issued orders to his division commanders to prepare for evacuation that night. His instructions included plans for withdrawing the field artillery from the gun emplacements, assisted by details of infantry assigned by each division commander. To ensure the orderly withdrawal of his four infantry divisions, Johnston specified the various streets each division would utilize to march toward the river crossings. Walker's division, for example, was instructed to form his troops "on the low ground east of town below the ruins of the Bowman House" (the present-day site of the Mississippi State Fairgrounds) via the first street north of the capitol (present-day Amite Street) and the two streets to the north. Loring's men would use the two or three avenues north of Walker. French's and Breckinridge's divisions, meanwhile, were to move along the streets immediately south of the capitol. Breckinridge would be the last division to withdraw. All four division commanders were instructed to pull in their skirmishers at 1:00 a.m. Unfortunately, a few Confederate pickets never got the word and were subsequently captured. Others took the opportunity to desert. On the whole, though, Johnston's detailed instructions worked admirably, and the "Army of Relief" was safely across the Pearl

River before sunrise, crossing on three pontoon bridges. To mask the noise of the withdrawal, Confederate bands, as they had done each night of the siege, played a number of patriotic tunes, including "Bonnie Blue Flag" and "Dixie," which, according to a soldier in the Forty-sixth Indiana, elicited cheers from both sides.[164]

Early the next morning, Lieutenant J. Wilson Ingell, an officer in the Thirty-fifth Massachusetts Infantry, crept toward the Confederate earthworks on the northern fringe of the city. The day seemed eerily quiet. During the night there had been signs that something was afoot, including reports that wagons were heard moving about. Many Federal soldiers also observed a glow inside the city. "A bright light appeared over the city," remembered a soldier in the Thirty-fifth Massachusetts, "the bells rang for fire and there was a great stir; then the glow died out and all was quiet." All these signs indicated that an evacuation might be underway by Johnston's army, but the Union high command remained unconvinced until the morning's light revealed that Johnston had indeed escaped.

The Old Capitol Museum, one of several prominent wartime structures in Jackson. *Photo by author.*

Creeping toward the lines, Ingell and others observed a black man standing on the parapet of the Cotton Bale Battery and waving a white flag. Sergeant Major Samuel Berry and an officer from the Forty-sixth New York subsequently learned that the city had indeed been abandoned. Rushing forward in order to be the first to enter Jackson, troops from Brigadier General Edward Ferrero's brigade won the race, and it was Berry who first entered the stately Mississippi Capitol. Climbing to the top of the building, Berry and several other men from the regiment exchanged the Confederate flag still floating above the building with the Stars and Stripes. Not to be outdone, soldiers from the Fifty-first Pennsylvania planted their flag in the front lawn of the capitol. For Ferrero's men, along with the rest of Parke's troops, the opportunity to be the first to enter Jackson was a badge of honor for the Easterners who had received much ribbing (good-natured and otherwise) from their counterparts in the XV and XIII Corps. "This feat was received by the Western troops with a very bad grace," wrote Captain Thomas Parker of the Fifty-first Pennsylvania. "It silenced their abuse against the 9th Army Corps."[165]

Almost as soon as Johnston had completed his withdrawal, Jackson's civil authorities appealed to Sherman for protection of the city. In a resolution passed by the Board of Aldermen, Mayor Charles Henry Manship, who was a decorative painter by trade, sent a communication to Sherman's headquarters under a flag of truce to ascertain the terms "on which your troops will occupy this place." In the resolution, Manship noted the condition of the city prior to the Federal occupation. "Already this place has suffered severely from the calamities of war," he wrote. "A large part of it is in ashes. Many families are without houses, and during the past week, nearly the whole population has been compelled to remove from their houses to avoid the dangers of a bombardment. We trust," he concluded, "that the citizens of this place will receive from you that usage which the laws of civilized warfare have established in such cases and that ample protection and security will be accorded to the women and children, and unarmed citizens, as well as to private property." A committee of twenty prominent citizens was also appointed to receive Sherman.[166] In response, Sherman assured the mayor that "all citizens acting in good faith will be respected by me and my command and that families will be encouraged to get home, stay there, and resume their peaceful vocations," though he could make no terms. Later, after meeting with members of the delegation, Sherman reported to Grant that these men "admit themselves beaten, subdued, and charge their rulers and agitators with bringing ruin and misery on the State" and that they had expressed their desire to begin the process of getting Mississippi readmitted to the Union. Seeing an opening, Sherman proposed to Grant an ambitious plan: the establishment of a trading depot on the Big Black River where loyal citizens of Mississippi could exchange cotton, corn or other products for the necessities of life. This, Sherman argued, might drive a wedge between the citizens and their Confederate masters and encourage the end of hostilities. Grant, however, declined Sherman's proposal, although he did approve a request by Mayor Manship for help in feeding the people of Jackson. To that end, Sherman ordered that two hundred barrels of flour and one hundred barrels of pork be distributed to the people of Jackson. Additional rations were provided to the citizens of Clinton.[167]

Despite Sherman's promises to the contrary, some of Parke's men celebrated their victory by looting many of the businesses and homes along State Street, although a guard was posted on the capitol grounds to prevent damage to the statehouse. Captain Thomas Parker of the Fifty-first Pennsylvania recalled that "private dwellings [were] entered and plundered of money, jewelry, and all else of any value was carried off; crockery, chinaware, pianos, furniture, &c., were smashed to atoms; hogsheads of sugar rolled into the street and the heads knocked in and contents spilled." Several members of the regiment even donned women's clothing and paraded through the streets "in the most laughable and grotesque habiliments that could be found." While thus attired, the regiment met its brigade commander, Ferrero, as well as Sherman. With "a severely stern look of anger on his countenance," Ferrero appeared ready to rebuke the men when one soldier, wearing "an old-fashioned, high-crowned Dunstable bonnet, saluted him with so much *sang froid* as to make him burst out in a peal of laughter that could not be controlled." Ferrero rode away "amid the cheers of the regiment."[168]

At noon, Sherman ordered Major General Frank Blair's division of Steele's XV Corps to move into Jackson and take charge of the city, relieving the men of the IX Corps. Their entrance into Jackson was delayed somewhat when a "mine"—an artillery shell planted in the road by Johnston's men—exploded, killing one man and wounding several others. These "torpedoes," described by one soldier as "most inhuman and diabolical," would serve as an excuse for additional looting by some. In an attempt to quell such behavior, Sherman directed Blair to "maintain order and good discipline within the limits of the place, repressing all pillage, plundering, and rowdyism." He also authorized Blair to collect all those "having no orders or business from proper authority" to work on destroying the railroad. With the exception of Blair's division

Edwin Chamberlain of the Eleventh New Hampshire was one of the IX Corps soldiers who came to Mississippi from the Eastern Theater. *Library of Congress.*

and an ad hoc force assembled to march toward Brandon, the rest of the XV Corps went into camp near the Deaf and Dumb Asylum west of town, while the IX Corps bivouacked near the Insane Asylum. The XIII Corps, meanwhile, camped along Lynch Creek near the Raymond Road.[169]

As his occupation troops moved into their assigned positions, Sherman examined the city he had just captured. Observing that the "enemy had…fired a building containing commissary stores," which then spread to consume "one of the most valuable blocks of the city," Sherman reported that Jackson "with the destruction committed by ourselves in May last and by the enemy during this siege, is one mass of charred ruins."[170] Sherman's blunt assessment was not the only eyewitness account regarding damage to the city. Indeed, numerous primary accounts by Union soldiers and civilians alike, including newspaper correspondents, reported extensive damage. As a result, Jackson would earn the sobriquet of "Chimneyville."

After touring the city, Sherman moved into the Governor's Mansion and made it his headquarters, where he hosted a victory dinner that night with his generals. Afterward, in a letter to his friend Admiral David Dixon Porter, Sherman reported that "we had a beautiful supper and union of the generals of the army" and that "the 'Army and Navy forever' was sung with a full and hearty chorus." Sherman also notified Grant that he had determined not to pursue Johnston due to the intense heat and lack of water. In response, Grant questioned Sherman's decision and inquired if he might use his cavalry to harass Johnston. Sherman, however, had no available cavalry, as they had been sent to wreck the railroads north and south of Jackson. Although Grant questioned Sherman's decision, he left the matter to his trusted subordinate. No doubt, this exchange irritated Sherman, but he decided to try and comply with Grant's wishes and ordered Steele to assemble a force to cross the river and pursue Johnston as far as Brandon, some fifteen miles east of Jackson.[171]

Steele's expeditionary force included Colonel Milo Smith's brigade and an ad hoc force composed of four regiments commanded by Colonel James Geddes. Steele's men began marching toward Brandon on the afternoon of July 18, crossing the river on a pontoon bridge erected by Union pioneers. At nightfall, the Federals bivouacked near a large Confederate hospital, where they found many of the wounded men from Lauman's attack on July 12. Meanwhile, Johnston continued marching east due to a shortage of water in the Brandon area, eventually halting west of Morton. To cover the retreating army, Cosby's cavalry was assigned to act as a rear guard. Cosby's men were joined by the rest of Jackson's cavalry in the evening, but due to a lack of forage, they continued farther east, leaving Cosby's brigade to watch for any developments. The weather, as it had been throughout the siege, was exceedingly hot.[172]

On the morning of July 19, Steele's men resumed the advance toward Brandon with Geddes's brigade in the front. Born in 1827, James Lorrain Geddes was a native of Edinburgh, Scotland. After service with the Canadian cavalry in Calcutta, India, where he studied at the British military academy, Geddes moved to Iowa just prior to the Civil War. Enlisting in the Eighth

Iowa as a private, he earned promotion to colonel by the spring of 1862 and during the Jackson Campaign served in Joseph J. Wood's brigade of Tuttle's division.[173] Approximately five miles from Brandon, Geddes' men ran into a Confederate outpost, which promptly retreated and informed Cosby that the Federals were on the march. Cosby, however, took no immediate action. In a short time, he was alerted that the Yankees were now much closer to Brandon. This time, Cosby snapped into action and ordered his dismounted troopers to form a defensive line on either side of the road. He also deployed the three guns of Clark's Missouri Battery, commanded by Captain Houston King. With his line established, Cosby sent word to Johnston that Union forces were advancing on Brandon, the first word Johnston had that any Union troops has crossed the Pearl. Almost immediately, Geddes emerged from the woods about a mile west of Cosby's position, and the fight was on. The Confederate artillerymen fired first, killing twenty-two-year-old Sergeant John Duncan of the Eighth Iowa, who was acting as an orderly sergeant. Faced with Confederate artillery, Geddes deployed his brigade in line of battle with the Seventy-second Ohio held in reserve. He also deployed Captain Allen C. Waterhouse's Battery E, First Illinois Light Artillery, to answer the Confederates. The Illinois battery had smoothbores, however, and were outgunned by the Missourians, who sported rifled Parrotts. Thus, they had better range and used the opportunity to pound Geddes's infantry. With his men taking unwelcome artillery fire, Geddes ordered the infantry forward. Advancing into a large cornfield east of the Miller house, Geddes's men had difficulty traversing the deep corn rows. Struggling toward Cosby's position, the Federals finally got within small arms range when the heavens opened up and soaked the combatants in a terrific downpour. Unable to advance until the rain eased, Cosby used the delay to beat a hasty retreat. With the road now clear, the Federals marched into Brandon, where they camped for the night.[174]

The county seat of Rankin County, Brandon had not yet been occupied by any Union troops, and according to Major David Reed of the Thirteenth Iowa, their arrival on this occasion "created considerable excitement and no little curiosity among the ladies of the place. Some of them," he wrote, "after viewing the soldiers through closed blinds, came out on the porch and became interested in a section of artillery planted in the street. One of them was heard to remark: 'I wish they would fire it, I'd like to hear it.'" At the next opportunity, the battery commander quietly ordered the gunner to fire the gun. "The shock of the discharge," wrote Reed, "shattered the window glass and sent the curious ones screaming into the house, their curiosity fully satisfied."[175] Unfortunately for the citizens of Brandon, Steele's visit would result in much greater destruction than a bit of broken glass. During the night, troops commanded by Colonel John W. King burned a quarter of the town and tried to burn the courthouse. According to the editor of the *Brandon Republican* newspaper, the Yankees swarmed into the town like a "gang of thieves" and robbed the people of "clothing, jewelry, wine, cordials, preserves, [and] pickles." The next morning, Steele's men tore up the railroad and burned the depot. After inflicting a great deal of damage, the Federals returned to Jackson, where they arrived on the evening of the twentieth.[176]

During Steele's expedition to Brandon, Sherman's forces had been busy with the serious work of destroying the captured supplies and railroad facilities in and around

James W. Atwood, a soldier in the Thirteenth Iowa Infantry, was one of Sherman's "western" men. *Wilson's Creek National Battlefield.*

Jackson, including demolition of the stone piers of the railroad bridge. The Union soldiers also dismantled and dumped the two 32-pounder guns left behind by Johnston. Another gun, a breech-loading rifled cannon, was transported to Vicksburg. Johnston also left behind in excess of twenty-three thousand rounds of ammunition, 1,400 rifles and stacks of infantry accoutrements, most of which was destroyed due to their inferior quality. The majority of work for Sherman's men, however, involved the destruction of the railroads radiating from the city. As was the case during the earlier occupation, the method of destroying the tracks involved prying up the rails and then heating and twisting them into a shape that would render them useless. Creating these "Sherman's neckties" was hard work, especially considering the extreme heat. Lieutenant George Elliott of the Ninety-seventh Indiana recalled that his brigade was ordered to march north and instructed to destroy the tracks for a distance of ten miles. "It is hot weather and hard labor," he wrote. "It seems that we do all the fighting and labor."[177] Brigadier General Alvin Hovey reported that his men destroyed more than five miles of track and twelve cars. In addition, they burned "a large quantity of timber and machinery." On July 20, the men of the Seventy-seventh Illinois marched to Byram, where a soldier in the regiment recalled that the Illinoisans "went to work and tore up some two or three miles more track, burning the ties and bending the rails which was pretty heavy work and by night we were very tired." After a hard day's work, the men feasted on peaches and corn taken from the surrounding farmland and then began the long march back to Jackson.[178]

After learning that Johnston's army had retreated farther to the east, Sherman decided it was time to begin moving his force back to Vicksburg. As such, all three corps commanders received instructions for the return march. The IX Corps was the first to leave, moving out on the morning of July 20. It took Parke's troops three days to trudge back to their camps on the west side of the Big Black. As might be expected, the march was exceedingly difficult, given the heat and lack of water. The XIII Corps marched out the next day and arrived in Vicksburg on the twenty-third. The XV Corps was the last to depart, finally moving out on the morning of July 23. After marching at a slow pace, Steele's men returned to their bivouacs on July 25.[179]

The Jackson Campaign and weeklong siege was finally over. For both Sherman's expeditionary force and Johnston's "Army of Relief," the extreme heat and lack of water were constant hardships, conditions that took a heavy toll on men in blue and gray. Compared to other Civil War actions, casualties were relatively light. During the expedition, Sherman suffered a total loss of 129 killed, 762 wounded and 231 missing, with most of the casualties suffered during Lauman's attack on July 12. Johnston, meanwhile, counted 71 killed, 504 wounded and 25 missing. All in all, both men seemed satisfied with the results. For Sherman, the campaign was "a fit supplement to the reconquest of the Mississippi River itself, and makes that perfect which otherwise would have been imperfect."[180] In other words, Sherman, in his first successful independent command, had just applied the finishing stroke to the Vicksburg Campaign. Johnston, meanwhile, could be proud of the way in which his men conducted themselves on the retreat to Jackson and during the siege, and the withdrawal—never an easy task—had been performed with skill. He could also be satisfied that, unlike Pemberton, he had saved his army for another day, an outcome lauded by several contemporary newspapers. While both commanders achieved a degree of satisfaction, the people of Jackson were left to pick up the pieces.

CHAPTER 7

"CHIMNEYVILLE"

For many years, the term "Chimneyville," which first appeared in a newspaper account written after the siege, has been associated with the damage inflicted on Jackson during the Civil War and has specifically been associated with Sherman. Even in modern times, "Chimneyville" remains a powerful metaphor, evoking images of burned buildings and total devastation. Many contemporary eyewitness accounts support in whole or in part the destruction that occurred in Jackson. For a number of years, however, some historians have questioned the actual extent of the damage, based in part on an 1869 photograph that appears to show a largely undamaged city. As is often the case, the truth of what took place in Jackson during the war is a complicated story.

Before examining what took place during and after the Siege of Jackson, it is important to note what occurred prior to July 1863. Following Mississippi's secession in 1861, Jackson, like most other cities in the South, began to feel the effects of war. Not only did the city's population swell with Confederate troops, but a number of the local industries converted to the production of war materiel. Examples include the Green brothers' textile mill, which produced tent cloth and other articles for the Confederate army, and a munitions factory, known as the Jackson Arsenal. Located a few blocks northeast of the state capitol, the arsenal exploded on the afternoon of November 5, 1862, killing dozens of men, women and children, their remains "blackened and disfigured so as to almost defy identity as human beings." The explosion produced a "fearful shock throughout the city and its suburbs," and scattered debris for hundreds of yards in all directions. Incredibly, a fire broke out the same night at a commercial establishment on the south end of town. Fanned by a strong wind, the flames swept across at least four other buildings and burned the Southern Railroad depot before finally being extinguished. With the fire brigade already overwhelmed by the arsenal building disaster, a portion of Jackson's business district suffered a considerable loss in the fire. The debris from the arsenal explosion remained unattended for quite some time.[181]

In May 1863, Union forces first entered Jackson and briefly occupied the city. During that occupation, a number of structures were burned, including railroad facilities, a foundry and machine shop, the aforementioned Green brothers' mill, and the state penitentiary, which had also been converted to military production. Along with these obvious military targets, several other buildings were torched, including the Catholic church and the Confederate Hotel, neither of which can be justified militarily. There were also accounts of widespread looting, despite the fact that Sherman made a point of ordering Brigadier General Joseph Mower to curtail such activities. Following the May occupation of the city, Sherman wrote that "Jackson, as a railroad center or Government depot of stores and military factories,

In this illustration from *Harper's Weekly*, the top image shows some of the destruction in Jackson on May 15. The bottom illustration is of the battle of Champion Hill. *Mississippi Department of Archives and History.*

can be of little use to the enemy for six months," and Lieutenant Colonel Arthur Freemantle, the British observer, noted that "the whole town was a miserable wreck, and presented a deplorable aspect."[182] Less than a month later, on June 10, 1863, yet another tragedy struck, this time to the largest hotel in Jackson. The Bowman House went up in flames at about 3:00 a.m. "So rapid was the progress of the flames," reported the *Daily Mississippian*, "that in fifteen minutes from its discovery the entire roof on both wings fell in, and ten minutes later the upper story was in flames." Once regarded as among Mississippi's finest, the hotel was a complete loss. Significantly, the ruins of the hotel, located on a prominent corner in Jackson, remained until 1874. Thus, several months before the siege, Jackson had already suffered a significant amount of damage.[183]

One month after the Bowman House fire, of course, Johnston's and Sherman's armies faced each other across Jackson's siege lines. During the weeklong conflict, there were reports of damage from Union bombardments, and a number of houses situated between the lines were burned to establish fields of fire. According to one account, there was also looting of private property during the siege by at least some Confederate troops. On July 14, Lieutenant J.M. Armstrong of the Lookout (Tennessee) Battery wrote to his sister that "the city is a perfect waste. All the citizens gone. Their fine fences have been torn down for shelters and all the gardens is our common pasture. A great many houses have been broken open & ransacked by our men & everything that is valuable taken away. I am perfectly disgusted with such conduct. The citizens say they were not ½ so much damaged by the federals while they stayed here."[184] A similar sentiment was expressed in Canton, where the editor of the *Canton American Citizen* reported, "A portion of Jackson's [cavalry] command was a lawless, violent, insubordinate set of men. They pillaged and robbed our stores, and murdered one of our best citizens." Fearing the same fate would result from the Federal army, the editor was pleasantly surprised. "The treatment of our citizens generally by the Yankees," he wrote, "was not so bad as had been anticipated. Here in town they entered but few dwellings, and committed but few depredations."[185]

After Johnston's evacuation of Jackson and the subsequent occupation of the city by Sherman's men, more eyewitness accounts describe widespread looting and other vandalism. The largest number of these accounts come from Union soldiers themselves. Henry Tisdale, a solider in the Thirty-fifth Massachusetts Infantry, was among the first soldiers to enter the city on July 17. In his memoir, Tisdale wrote that "most of the stores had been cleared out and what of them had not were soon ransacked of whatever could be of use to us. Sugar and molasses were found in considerable quantities, casks of which were rolled into the streets, heads knocked out and we were soon rolling in sweets." In addition, he noted that "many houses showed the effects of our shells, in smashed rooks, demolished chimneys, etc."[186] George Whitman, a soldier in the Fifty-first New York Infantry and the younger brother of the famed poet Walt Whitman, reported the plundering in Jackson but blamed the damage on the "western" troops of the army. "Soon after we entered," he wrote, "the western troops began to come in, and they ransacked and plundered…completely."[187] On July 18, a member of the Chicago Mercantile Battery had the opportunity to visit the city and found that it was "an example of ruin and desolation. Block after block of stores have been burned. Residences torn to pieces. Public buildings in ruins and all a blackened mess."[188] Likewise, Charles Wilcox of the Thirty-third Illinois observed a great deal of pillaging and fires set by fellow soldiers. "I never saw or heard of a city being so thoroughly sacked and burned as this place," he wrote. "It is indeed a great pity that so fine a city should be so destroyed."[189] Thomas Linn, a drummer in the Sixteenth Ohio, also reported that the town was in ashes and added a much more gruesome detail. After visiting the city with a comrade on the afternoon of the seventeenth, Linn "saw the ashes of a human body which had been burned" and added that a shell in a building exploded and killed a couple of men.[190] Curiously, Captain Peter Casey of the Ninetieth Illinois reported that Jackson's "houses were all destroyed, Statehouse and all. I do not think there is six houses left standing in Jackson which I think is wrong." Despite his note about the capitol, the building suffered no appreciable damage.[191] Numerous other Federal soldier accounts survive, and each one follows a similar theme.

Newspaper accounts are another rich source. These reports were often filed by correspondents who were present with the army and who made personal observations on the ground. For example, a correspondent for the *New York Herald* was able to follow squads of troops as they entered the Confederate works and into town, despite orders to remain in their camps. "As our men would reach private dwelling houses they would enter them," he wrote, "and in a short time scenes of the most unmitigated plundering took place." Once Blair's division entered town, he reported that much of the looting ended but also noted that "the rebels burned up fifty or sixty buildings on the street fronting the Capitol" in order to destroy large quantities of army stores. "The day was sultry, scarcely a current of fresh air being felt, and the smoke from the ruins of the fires coursed along through the principal streets, making a trip through the city decidedly

Union major general Francis P. Blair Jr. *Wilson's Creek National Battlefield.*

unpleasant."[192] Likewise, a reporter for the *Memphis Bulletin* (a former Whig newspaper that favored the Union), provided graphic details of Jackson's demise. "The scene in the suburbs of the city in the morning ere the main army had entered the town, was most disgraceful," he wrote. "Lazy, lousy, filthy, contemptible stragglers…could be seen in every old alley and back street, engaged in dividing their ill-gotten plunder, which consisted of fine silks, shoes, ladies bonnets…My pen can never record what of outrage was done that day." After recounting a long list of properties that had been burned, including the telegraph office, the *Weekly Mississippian*, the Episcopal Church, a confectioner's shop, several law offices and a large restaurant, the reporter for the *Bulletin* wrote "the rebellious city seemed one solid sheet of fire. From building to building leaped the lambent flames—the streets were crowded with household paraphernalia, carpets, mirrors, melodeons—weeping women sat beside their perishing property with hair disheveled and implored the gods to save them—little children ran the streets in wild despair, invoking the names of father and mother—a perfect bedlam of fire bells rent the insuspicious heavens."[193] Not to be outdone by their Northern counterparts, the *Charleston Mercury* reported on July 31 that "in Jackson nearly all of Main street [State Street], the Governor's mansion, and many other houses, were burned to the ground" and that the "soldiers pillaged every house, and stole whatever they could lay their hands on." Clearly, this account, which was not based on an eyewitness, got a significant fact wrong: the Governor's Mansion, used by Sherman as his headquarters, was not harmed to any great degree, although individual soldiers did take some items from the Governor's Mansion as souvenirs, among them Samuel McQuade, the principal musician of the Twenty-seventh Michigan Infantry, who somehow managed to carry a stolen vase in his knapsack throughout the remainder of the war.[194] Incredibly, one correspondent visited Jackson while Sherman's troops were still engaged in the destruction of the railroad. Based on this eyewitness account, the following item appeared in the *Canton American Citizen*:

> *One must visit Jackson to learn the extent of the destruction it has sustained. It is a mere wreck of its former self. To give you an account of what was the business part of the city, I will inform you that, from the Bowman House, including that fine hotel, to the freight depot of the Vicksburg railroad, there are not ten buildings left standing upon both sides* [of] *State street. The same is the case upon the streets leading from State street to the New Orleans railroad* [Capitol Street], *and look in whichever direction you may from the front of the Capitol, ruins meet the eye. The numerous chimneys still standing upon burnt districts, and the undisturbed debris of charred walls and destroyed wares, will remain until the end of the war, silent but terrible monuments of the devastating inroad of the vandal horde who, laying waste our homes and our altars, would insult our manhood by inviting us again to live with them under the same flag as brethren.*[195]

Continuing, the correspondent listed other specific buildings, including several private residences, that had been burned or looted but also acknowledged that, to his surprise, the "vandal horde" had not burned the state capitol. Significantly, the account includes structures that had already been lost prior to the siege, including the Bowman House, which had burned by accident in June.

Following the departure of Sherman's troops, it took several weeks for additional reporters to enter Jackson, due to the condition of the roads and rail lines. One of the first who did so was a correspondent for the *Memphis Daily Appeal*. In a remarkable series of reports filed in mid-August, the *Appeal*'s correspondent, who happened to be a former resident of Jackson, wrote extensively about the city and the surrounding area. On August 21, he reported:

> *Jackson is a dreary looking place. The business portion of the city, with the exception of a few stores on Cheapside, is all in ashes. Most of the private residences near the line of battle, being unoccupied when the enemy took possession, were pillaged and destroyed. I entered Jackson at night, and as I passed up State street, the scene was, indeed, calculated to arouse sad and bitter emotions in the breast of one who has been want to regard it as the "dearest spot on earth" to him. Chimneys and broken walls now only*

This image shows the ruins of the Bowman House hotel, which burned in June 1863, in the foreground. The state capitol is in the background. *Mississippi Department of Archives and History.*

remain where, but a few months since, the speculator, the honest tradesman and the Government official found shelter in elegant stores and commodious offices. While the destruction of so much valuable property is to be deplored, the incendiary torch accomplished some good. "Greasy Row," and other rows of debauch and crime, are no longer institutions of Jackson. They are gone, and Heaven forbid their return. Two churches have been destroyed by the vandals—the Catholic and Episcopal. The State house and Executive mansion were not damaged further than the destruction of some books in the upper library of the former, and I presume, some pillaging of the latter.

Interestingly, the *Appeal*'s correspondent affirmed in his report that Johnston's retreating army started some of the fires in order to destroy provisions that could be carried away. The fires, he wrote, were "started by our own men—whether acting under orders or not, I cannot say."[196]

In addition to eyewitness accounts from soldiers and newspaper correspondents, there were a number of individuals whose accounts provide further evidence regarding Jackson's condition. Among them is the grand master of Mississippi's Masonic lodges, Richard Cooper. In January 1864, Mississippi's Grand Lodge met in Columbus. At that gathering, Cooper, as the the grand master, reported on the state of Freemasonry throughout the state, including the number of lodges that had been destroyed during the war. In his report, Cooper stated, "Hitherto it has been the practice among civilized nations at war, to respect the property, furniture and jewels of Masonic Lodges, and instances are on record—where such things were captured, they were promptly restored with due courtesy." In Jackson, however, Cooper reported that "it was reserved for the armies of the United States, when they occupied the city of Jackson, to invade the sanctity of the Hall of the Grand Lodge, and other Masonic bodies, and the offices thereof, and wantonly to destroy the furniture, records and archives of the Grand Lodge." After visiting the city a few days after the evacuation of Sherman's troops, Cooper found that the city was "a scene of destruction and demolition."[197] Likewise, Bishop William Elder of the Catholic Diocese of Natchez was allowed to pass through the lines from Brandon, where he had been attending to wounded troops in the field hospitals and entered Jackson on July 20, where he found nothing but "melancholy desolation." In May, the Catholic church, then located on Court Street, had been burned by Federal troops. Now, he found that the temporary church, located in the Spengler's Saloon, had also been burned and the chalice and crucifix had been stolen (although they were later returned). The city itself, he observed, was in desperate shape. "The sight of Jackson is indeed saddening," he wrote. "Perhaps one fourth of the town is in ashes.—Some entire blocks & many single houses. All the stores are broken open & sacked. They were carrying off boxes that seem to contain books of the State House Library. Some of the people of Jackson are still in the woods where they took refuge during the bombardment…There is nothing in town to eat: all the neighborhood is desolated:—from a distance nothing can be brought. There are no teams & no roads—no bridges. The policy seems to make Jackson untenable, for soldiers or civilians."[198] Finally, Jackson's mayor, Charles Manship, who had appealed to Sherman to protect private property even as Johnston's army was in the process of evacuating the city, described Jackson's "lamentable state" in the Minutes of the Board of Aldermen on August 7. In that document, Manship reported "scenes of wanton destruction [and] spoilation" and "general and indiscriminate plunder, burning, and destruction" which had occurred during the Federal occupation in July. Manship submitted the report, which was very critical of Sherman, to correct the notion that the city leaders had not done enough to try to protect the city's assets. He wrote:

> *I have thought it advisable to make this report and submit it to you, because of the expression given to opinions by some of our citizens, after the first occupation of our City by the federals, to the effect, that "something ought to have been done by the City authorities at that time by way of communication with the Federals to obtain protection and avert the calamities then endured."; also, to make public the fact that such a course has been adopted in this second visitation of our enemies and the results of such a course: as well as that all the facts herein set forth may become [a] matter of history in the Records of Jackson as it passed through the fiery ordeal of Civil War.*[199]

Finally, there is documentary evidence available among the advertisements and business listings published in the newspapers of the period. In 1860, John Logan Power, a native of Ireland and a local newspaper editor and printer, published Jackson's first city directory, which listed all of the public institutions, churches, schools, hotels, manufacturers and businesses located throughout the capital city. In all, approximately 140 establishments were included. Of these, the largest category were law offices, with twenty-three attorneys located in Jackson. There were also 10 hotels and boardinghouses, including the Bowman House.[200] In January 1866, Power again published a city directory with similar categories of business listings. This time, however, less than 40 businesses remained in the directory, including just 2 hotels listed (the Dickson House and "Mrs. Flusser's House of Entertainment," located on Tombigbee Street). Of these, the Dickson House advertised that it had been "thoroughly cleaned, and repaired, and fitted with entirely new furniture." The firm of Spengler & Zehnder, dealer in "Havana Cigars, Tobacco & Fruits," had been rebuilt and was back in business at the corner of State and Capitol Streets. Nearby were 2 saloons, 1 of which was appropriately named the Phoenix. There were just 2 attorney offices remaining, a precipitous decline perhaps attributable to the absence of the state government as much as the calamity of war. By comparing all of the listings, however, it seems clear that Jackson saw a significant decline in businesses and other establishments during the war, although economic ruin and the general conditions present could account for some of the loss.[201]

Given the number of eyewitness accounts and other primary evidence, there can be little doubt that Jackson indeed suffered significant damage during the Civil War, whether as a result of Federal occupation, unintended and accidental disasters, the planned burning of houses between the lines by Confederate troops or looting by soldiers of both armies. Despite this, it is also clear that not all of Jackson was destroyed, as the term "Chimneyville" might indicate. As previously noted, both the Governor's Mansion and the state capitol were largely unharmed. In addition, both the city hall and

The home of Jackson's mayor during the siege, Charles Manship, survived the war and is now a house museum. *Library of Congress.*

the Insane Asylum escaped significant damage. The Presbyterian church, located a short distance from the Bowman House ruins, also remained undamaged. Based on data collected by architectural historians, it is evident that numerous antebellum homes once lined North State Street in the postwar years, many of which survived well into the twentieth century. Today, approximately a dozen antebellum structures remain in Jackson, including the Manship House and the Oaks House, both of which belonged to mayors of Jackson.[202]

If it is true that Jackson suffered significant damage during the war, and if it is true that a substantial number of antebellum buildings—particularly among residential structures—survived, it is logical to assume that Jackson's citizens rebuilt their city and repaired the damage. Indeed, advertisements from the immediate postwar period indicate that businesses returned to the capital city at a rapid pace. In May 1866, gas lighting was restored, showing that civil authorities were also making efforts to restore Jackson's infrastructure. According to a contemporary newspaper account, "the improvements now going on in our city speak well for the energy and perseverance of its citizens. Stores are going up in all parts of the town." While the writer noted that "there are not as many dwelling houses going up as we would wish to see," there were many existing residences being refurbished. "Fences are being repaired" the writer continued, "outbuildings rebuilt, the shrubbery trimmed, and the gardens are receiving the care necessary to their putting on their spring dress of richness, beauty and fragrance."[203] By the end of 1866, "Chimneyville" seemed to be on the mend.

In 1869, a local photographer named Elisaeus von Seutter climbed to the cupola of the state capitol to take a panoramic image of Jackson. Born in Germany in 1827, von Seutter moved from nearby Raymond to Jackson after the war and established a successful jewelry, watchmaker and photography studio. The photograph he took in 1869 shows an expanding (but still somewhat rural) city, with a substantial number of structures clearly fronting State Street opposite the capitol, including a two-story "Spengler's Corner" building. Also visible is city hall, the Presbyterian church, the Christian church and the ruins of the Bowman House, among other identifiable structures. In the distance, both the burned-out state penitentiary (where the current state capitol is now located) and Mayor Charles Manship's house (now a local museum) are clearly visible. This remarkable photograph, taken four years after the Civil War, serves as documentary evidence of Jackson's growth and development in the immediate postwar years. The photograph has also for many years caused doubts about the extent of damage that actually took place in Jackson during the war. Based on the overwhelming number of primary accounts and the evidence of rebuilding found in newspapers of the period, it seems clear, however, that von Seutter's photograph shows a city in the process of being reborn.[204]

In 2005, Hurricane Katrina struck the Mississippi Gulf Coast with a fury and caused a tremendous amount of damage. Initial reports from eyewitnesses indicated that the coastal counties suffered almost complete devastation, and it seemed that almost nothing remained on the coastline. While the devastation was indeed catastrophic, there were, in fact, buildings that survived the storm, including Beauvoir, the postwar home of Confederate president Jefferson Davis. While heavily damaged, Beauvoir, as first reports seemed to indicate, was not lost after all. It is perhaps part of human nature to witness the effects of a disaster, whether natural or man-made, and to see nothing but total devastation. Likely, it is part of being in shock over the loss of a community. Over time, however, it is often the case that further investigation reveals that not everything was destroyed and that, in fact, there are buildings that can be restored. Such is certainly the case following

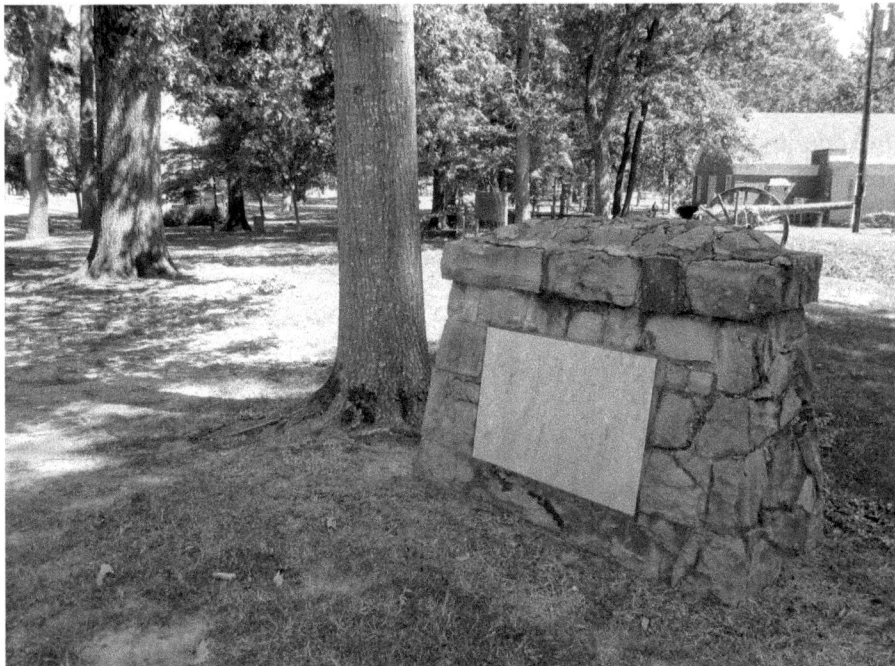

Battlefield Park, located near Highway 80 in Jackson, contains earthworks erected by Union troops during the siege, although they are misidentified as Confederate trenches. *Photo by author.*

Hurricane Katrina, thanks to the hard work and perseverance of local citizens, public officials and dedicated preservationists. In considering the story of Jackson, this also seems to be the case. Despite the initial reports of complete and total devastation, Jackson's citizens over time were able to rebuild and restore their city. It is this story—one of rebirth and renewal—that is perhaps more compelling and of greater value than the story of fire and destruction during the war.

Modern Jackson has since grown by leaps and bounds and is the largest metropolitan area in Mississippi. Unfortunately, the battlefield upon which Johnston's and Sherman's men fought in the summer of 1863 has largely been lost and few physical reminders of the siege remain. Those that do remain include a battery position on the campus of the University of Mississippi Medical Center, a section of Union earthworks constructed by Hovey's division at "Battlefield Park" near Highway 80 and the remnants of gun emplacements and trenches on top of "Bailey's Hill" south of Interstate 20. Of course, some of the antebellum structures also remain, including the Old Capitol Museum. In addition to these sites, the terrain and street network of downtown Jackson has not changed to such a degree that the battlefield cannot be understood, and there are areas throughout Jackson where interpretation could be used to explain what took place. Such an effort would in some small way help in remembering the sacrifices made by the men in blue and gray during those hot days in July 1863. We owe them nothing less.

Union Order of Battle

Army of the Tennessee, Expeditionary Army

Major General William T. Sherman

IX Army Corps

Major General John Grubb Parke

First Division

Brigadier General Thomas Welsh

First Brigade—Colonel Henry Bowman
36th Massachusetts Infantry—Lieutenant Colonel John B. Norton
17th Michigan Infantry—Lieutenant Colonel Constant Luce
27th Michigan Infantry—Colonel Dorus M. Fox
45th Pennsylvania Infantry—Colonel John I. Curtin

Third Brigade—Colonel Daniel Leasure
2nd Michigan Infantry—Colonel William Humphrey

8th Michigan Infantry—Colonel Frank Graves
20th Michigan Infantry—Lieutenant Colonel W. Huntington Smith
79th New York Infantry—Colonel David Morrison
100th Pennsylvania Infantry—Lieutenant Colonel Matthew M. Dawson

First Division Artillery
    Battery D, Pennsylvania Light Artillery—Captain George Washington Durell
    Battery L & M, 3rd United States Artillery—Captain John Edwards Jr.

Second Division

Brigadier General Robert Brown Potter

First Brigade—Colonel Simon Goodell Griffin
6th New Hampshire Infantry—Lieutenant Colonel Henry H. Pearson
9th New Hampshire Infantry—Colonel Herbert Bradwell Titus
7th Rhode Island Infantry—Colonel Zenas Randall Bliss

Second Brigade—Brigadier General Edward Ferrero
35th Massachusetts Infantry—Lieutenant Colonel R. Carlton Mitchell (51st New York)
11th New Hampshire Infantry—Lieutenant Colonel Moses N. Collins
51st New York Infantry—Colonel Charles William Joseph Emile Le Gendre
51st Pennsylvania Infantry—Colonel John Frederick Hartranft

Third Brigade—Colonel Benjamin C. Christ/Colonel Joseph Gerhardt
29th Massachusetts Infantry—Lieutenant Colonel Joseph H. Barnes
46th New York Infantry—Colonel Joseph Gerhardt/Lieutenant Colonel George W. Travers
50th Pennsylvania Infantry—Lieutenant Colonel Thomas Severn Brenholtz/Major Edward Overton Jr.

Second Division Artillery
    Battery L, 2nd New York Light Artillery—Captain Jacob Roemer
    Battery E, 2nd United States Artillery—Lieutenant Samuel N. Benjamin

APPENDIX A

First Division (XVI Corps)

Brigadier General William Sooy Smith

First Brigade—Colonel John Mason Loomis
26th Illinois Infantry—Lieutenant Colonel Robert A. Gilmore
90th Illinois Infantry—Colonel Timothy O'Meara
12th Indiana Infantry—Colonel Reuben Williams
100th Indiana Infantry—Lieutenant Colonel Albert Heath

Second Brigade—Colonel Stephen G. Hicks
40th Illinois Infantry—Major Hiram W. Hall
103rd Illinois Infantry—Colonel Willard A. Dickerman
15th Michigan Infantry—Colonel John Morrison Oliver
46th Ohio Infantry—Colonel Charles C. Walcutt

Third Brigade—Colonel Joseph R. Cockerill
97th Indiana Infantry—Colonel Robert Francis Catterson
99th Indiana Infantry—Colonel Alexander Fowler
53rd Ohio Infantry—Colonel Wells S. Jones
70th Ohio Infantry—Major William B. Brown

Fourth Brigade—Colonel William W. Sanford
48th Illinois Infantry—Lieutenant Colonel Lucien Greathouse
6th Iowa Infantry—Colonel John Murray Corse

First Division Artillery—Captain William Cogswell
1st Illinois Light Artillery, Company F—Captain John T. Cheney
1st Illinois Light Artillery, Company I—Lieutenant William N. Lansing
Cogswell's Battery, Illinois Light Artillery—Lieutenant Henry G. Eddy
6th Battery, Indiana Light Artillery—Captain Michael Muller

Cavalry Brigade—Colonel Cyrus Bussey
5th Illinois Cavalry—Major Thomas A. Apperson
3rd Iowa Cavalry (six companies)—Major Oliver Hazard Perry Scott
4th Iowa Cavalry—Colonel Edward Francis Winslow
2nd Wisconsin Cavalry (seven companies)—Colonel Thomas Stephens

Appendix A

XIII Army Corps

Major General Edward Otho Cresap Ord

Ninth Division

Brigadier General Peter Joseph Osterhaus

First Brigade—Colonel James Keigwin
49th Indiana Infantry—Major Arthur J. Hawhe
69th Indiana Infantry—Lieutenant Colonel Oran Perry
7th Kentucky Infantry—Colonel Reuben May
120th Ohio—Colonel Marcus M. Spiegel

Second Brigade—Colonel Daniel Lindsey
54th Indiana Infantry—Colonel Fielding Mansfield
22nd Kentucky Infantry—Lieutenant Colonel George Wood Monroe
16th Ohio Infantry—Major Milton Mills
42nd Ohio Infantry—Major William H. Williams

Cavalry Brigade—Major Hugh Fullerton
2nd Illinois Cavalry (three companies)—Major Benjamin Franklin Marsh
3rd Illinois Cavalry (three companies)—Colonel John L. Campbell
118th Illinois Mounted Infantry—Colonel John Giles Fonda
4th Indiana Cavalry (one company)—Captain Andrew P. Gallagher
6th Missouri Cavalry (seven companies)—Major Samuel Bacon Montgomery

Division Artillery—Captain Charles H. Lanphere
7th Michigan Light Artillery—Lieutenant George L. Stillman
1st Battery, Wisconsin Light Artillery—Lieutenant Oscar F. Nutting

Tenth Division

Brigadier General Andrew Jackson Smith

First Brigade—Colonel Richard Owen
16th Indiana Infantry—Captain Columbus Moore

60th Indiana Infantry—Major Jesse Nash
67th Indiana Infantry—Lieutenant Colonel Theodore E. Buehler
83rd Ohio Infantry—Lieutenant Colonel William Henry Baldwin
96th Ohio Infantry—Colonel Joseph W. Vance
23rd Wisconsin Infantry—Lieutenant Colonel William Freeman Vilas

Second Brigade—Colonel William Jennings Landrum
77th Illinois Infantry—Colonel David P. Grier
97th Illinois Infantry—Lieutenant Colonel Lewis D. Martin
130th Illinois Infantry—Colonel Nathaniel Niles
19th Kentucky Infantry—Lieutenant Colonel John W. Cowan
48th Ohio Infantry—Colonel Peter John Sullivan

Tenth Division Artillery
Chicago Mercantile Battery, Illinois Light Artillery—Captain Patrick H. White
17th Battery, Ohio Light Artillery—Captain Charles S. Rice

Twelfth Division

Brigadier General Alvin Peterson Hovey

First Brigade—Colonel William T. Spicely
11th Indiana Infantry—Lieutenant Colonel William W. Darnall
24th Indiana Infantry—Major John F. Grill
34th Indiana Infantry—Colonel Robert Alexander Cameron
46th Indiana Infantry—Colonel Thomas H. Bringhurst
29th Wisconsin Infantry—Lieutenant Colonel William A. Greene

Second Brigade—Colonel James Richard Slack
87th Illinois Infantry—Lieutenant Colonel John Montgomery Crebs
47th Indiana Infantry—Lieutenant Colonel John A. McLaughlin
24th Iowa Infantry—Lieutenant Colonel John Quincy Wilds
28th Iowa Infantry—Colonel John Connell
56th Ohio Infantry—Colonel William H. Raynor

Twelfth Division Artillery
1st Missouri Light Artillery, Company A—Lieutenant C.M. Callahan

2nd Battery, Ohio Light Artillery—Lieutenant Augustus Beach
16th Ohio Independent Battery—Lieutenant Russell P. Twist

Fourteenth Division

Brigadier General William Plummer Benton

First Brigade—Colonel David Shunk
93rd Illinois Infantry—Captain Isaac Hughes Elliott
99th Illinois Infantry—Lieutenant Colonel Lemuel Parke
8th Indiana Infantry—Major Thomas J. Brady
18th Indiana Infantry—Captain Jonathan H. Williams
1st Battery, Indiana Light Artillery—Lieutenant Philip Nonweiler

Second Brigade—Brigadier General Michael Kelly Lawler/Colonel
    William Milo Stone
21st Iowa Infantry—Major Salue Gattshall Van Anda
22nd Iowa Infantry—Captain Charles N. Lee
23rd Iowa Infantry—Major Leonard B. Houston
11th Wisconsin Infantry—Lieutenant Colonel Luther Holley Whittlesey
2nd Illinois Light Artillery, Company A—Lieutenant Frank B. Fenton

Fourth Division (XVI Corps)

Brigadier General Jacob Gartner Lauman/Brigadier General Alvin
    Peterson Hovey

First Brigade—Colonel Isaac Pugh
41st Illinois Infantry—Lieutenant Colonel John H. Nale/Major Frank
    M. Long
53rd Illinois Infantry—Lieutenant Colonel Seth C. Earl
3rd Iowa Infantry—Colonel Aaron Brown
33rd Wisconsin Infantry—Colonel Jonathan Baker Moore

Second Brigade—Colonel Cyrus Hall
14th Illinois Infantry—Lieutenant Colonel John J. Jones
15th Illinois Infantry—Lieutenant Colonel James Rany

46th Illinois Infantry—Colonel Benjamin Dornblaser
76th Illinois Infantry—Colonel Samuel Thompson Busey
53rd Indiana Infantry—Colonel Walter Quintin Gresham

Third Brigade—Colonel George Edwin Bryant
28th Illinois Infantry—Major Hinman Rhodes
32nd Illinois Infantry—Colonel John Logan
12th Wisconsin Infantry—Captain Giles Stevens

Fourth Division Artillery—Captain George Conrad Gumbart
2nd Illinois Light Artillery, Company E—Lieutenant George L. Nispel
2nd Illinois Light Artillery, Company K—Captain Benjamin Franklin Rodgers
5th Battery, Ohio Light Artillery—Lieutenant Anthony B. Burton
7th Battery, Ohio Light Artillery—Captain Silas Aeson Burnap
15th Battery Ohio Light Artillery—Captain Edward Spear Jr.

Cavalry
15th Illinois Cavalry, Companies F and I—Major James Grant Wilson

XV Corps

Major General Frederick Steele

First Division

Brigadier General John Milton Thayer

First Brigade—Colonel Bernard G. Farrar
13th Illinois Infantry – Colonel Adam B. Gorgas
27th Missouri Infantry—Colonel Thomas Curly
29th Missouri Infantry—Colonel James Peckham
30th Missouri Infantry—Lieutenant Colonel Otto Schadt
31st Missouri Infantry—Lieutenant Colonel Samuel P. Simpson
32nd Missouri Infantry—Major Abraham Jefferson Seay

Second Brigade—Colonel Charles Robert Woods
25th Iowa Infantry—Colonel George Augustus Stone
31st Iowa Infantry—Major Theore Stimming
3rd Missouri Infantry—Lieutenant Colonel Theodore M. Meumann
12th Missouri Infantry—Colonel Hugo Aurelius von Wangelin
17th Missouri Infantry—Major Francis Romer
76th Ohio—Lieutenant Colonel William Burnham Woods

Third Brigade—Colonel Milo Smith
4th Iowa Infantry—Lieutenant Colonel George Burton
9th Iowa Infantry—Colonel David Carskaddon
26th Iowa Infantry—Lieutenant Colonel Thomas George Ferreby
30th Iowa Infantry—Lieutenant Colonel William M.G. Torrence

First Division Artillery
1st Battery, Iowa Light Artillery—Captain Henry Holcomb Griffiths
2nd Missouri Light Artillery, Company F—Lieutenant Louis Voelkner
4th Battery, Ohio Light Artillery—Captain Louis Hoffmann

First Division Cavalry
Kane County (Illinois) Cavalry (Company)—Lieutenant Thomas Jefferson Beebe
3rd Illinois Cavalry, Company D—Lieutenant Jonathan Kershner

Second Division

Major General Francis Preston Blair Jr.

First Brigade—Colonel Giles Alexander Smith
113th Illinois Infantry—Lieutenant Colonel John Williams Paddock
116th Illinois Infantry—Colonel Nathan W. Tupper
6th Missouri Infantry—Colonel James Harvey Blood
8th Missouri Infantry—Lieutenant Colonel David Crockett Coleman
13th United States Infantry Battalion—Captain Charles C. Smith

Second Brigade—Brigadier General Joseph Andrew Jackson Lightburn
55th Illinois Infantry—Colonel Oscar Malmborg
127th Illinois Infantry—Colonel Hamilton N. Eldridge
83rd Indiana Infantry—Colonel Benjamin J. Spooner

54th Ohio Infantry—Lieutenant Colonel Cyrus W. Fisher
57th Ohio Infantry—Lieutenant Colonel Samuel R. Mott

Third Brigade—Brigadier General Hugh Boyle Ewing
30th Ohio Infantry—Colonel Theodore Jones
37th Ohio Infantry—Colonel Edward Siber
47th Ohio Infantry—Colonel Augustus Commodore Parry
4th West Virginia Infantry—Colonel James H. Dayton

Second Division Artillery
1st Illinois Light Artillery Company A—Captain Peter P. Wood
1st Illinois Light Artillery, Company B—Lieutenant Israel Parsons Rumsey
1st Illinois Light Artillery, Company H—Captain Levi W. Hart
8th Battery, Ohio Light Artillery—Captain James F. Putnam

Cavalry
Thielemann's (Illinois) Battalion, Companies A and B—Captain Milo
    Thielemann
10th Missouri Cavalry, Company C—Lieutenant Benjamin Joel

Third Division

Brigadier General James Madison Tuttle

First Brigade—Colonel William Linn McMillen
114th Illinois Infantry—Colonel John W. King
93rd Indiana Infantry—Colonel De Witt Clinton Thomas
72nd Ohio Infantry—Captain Samuel A.J. Snyder
95th Ohio Infantry—Lieutenant Colonel Jefferson Brumback

Third Brigade—Colonel Joseph Jackson Woods
8th Iowa Infantry—Colonel James Lorraine Geddes/Major William Stubbs
12th Iowa Infantry—Lieutenant Colonel Samuel R. Edgington
35th Iowa Infantry—Colonel Sylvester Gardner Hill

Division Artillery
1st Illinois Light Artillery, Company E—Captain Allen C. Waterhouse
2nd Battery, Iowa Light Artillery—Lieutenant Joseph Rea Reed

XVI Corps

First Division

Brigadier General William Sooy Smith (See IX Corps)

Fourth Division

Brigadier General Jacob Lauman/Brigadier General Alvin P. Hovey (See XIII Corps)

XVII Corps

Provisional Division

Brigadier General John McArthur

Second Brigade, Third Division—Colonel Manning Ferguson Force
30th Illinois Infantry—Lieutenant Colonel Warren Shedd
20th Ohio Infantry—Captain Francis Marion Shaklee
68th Ohio Infantry—Colonel Robert Kingston Scott
78th Ohio Infantry—Lieutenant Colonel Greenbury F. Wiles

Third Brigade, Sixth Division—Colonel Alexander Chambers
11th Iowa Infantry—Colonel William Hall
13th Iowa Infantry—Colonel John Shane
15th Iowa Infantry—Colonel William Worth Belknap
16th Iowa Infantry—Lieutenant Colonel Addison Hiatt Sanders

Third Brigade, Seventh Division—Brigadier General Charles Leopold Matthies
93rd Illinois Infantry—Colonel Holden Putnam
5th Iowa Infantry—Colonel Jabez Banbury
10th Iowa Infantry—Colonel William E. Small
26th Missouri Infantry—Captain Benjamin Devor Dean

CONFEDERATE ORDER OF BATTLE

ARMY OF RELIEF

General Joseph Eggleston Johnston

Breckinridge's Division

Major General John Cabell Breckinridge

Adams's Brigade—Brigadier General Daniel Weisisger Adams
32nd Alabama Infantry—Lieutenant Colonel Henry "Harry" Maury
13th and 20th Louisiana Infantry (Consolidated)—Colonel Augustus Reichard
14th Louisiana Sharpshooters Battalion—Major John E. Austin
16th and 25th Louisiana Infantry (Consolidated)—Colonel Daniel C. Gober
19th Louisiana Infantry—Colonel Wesley Parker Winans

Helm's Brigade—Brigadier General Benjamin Hardin Helm
41st Alabama Infantry—Colonel Martin Luther Stansel
2nd Kentucky Infantry—Lieutenant Colonel James W. Hewitt
4th Kentucky Infantry—Colonel Joseph Preyer Nuckols
6th Kentucky Infantry—Lieutenant Colonel Martin Hardin Cofer
9th Kentucky Infantry—Colonel John William Caldwell

Stovall's Brigade—Brigadier General Marcellus Augustus Stovall
1st and 3rd Florida Infantry (Consolidated)—Colonel William Scott Dilworth
4th Florida Infantry—Colonel Edward Nathaniel Badger
47th Georgia Infantry—Colonel Gilbert William Martin Williams/Captain Joseph Smith Cone
60th North Carolina Infantry—Lieutenant Colonel James M. Ray

Division Artillery—Major Rice Evans Graves
5th Company, Washington Artillery—Captain Cuthbert Harrison Slocomb
Cobb's Kentucky Battery—Captain Robert Cobb
Johnston's (Tennessee) Artillery—Captain John W. Mebane

French's Division

Major General Samuel G. French

McNair's Brigade—Brigadier General Evander McNair
1st Arkansas Mounted Rifles (Dismounted)—Lieutenant Colonel Daniel Harris Reynolds
2nd Arkansas Mounted Rifles (Dismounted)—Colonel James Adams Williamson
4th Arkansas Infantry—Colonel Henry Gaston Bunn
25th and 31st Arkansas Infantry (Consolidated)—Colonel Thomas Hamilton McCray
39th North Carolina Infantry—Colonel David Coleman

Maxey's Brigade—Brigadier General Samuel Bell Maxey
4th Louisiana Infantry—Colonel Samuel Eugene Hunter
30th Louisiana Infantry Battalion—Lieutenant Colonel Thomas Shields
42nd Tennessee Infantry—Lieutenant Colonel Isaac Newton Hulme
46th and 55th Tennessee Infantry (Consolidated)—Lieutenant Colonel Gideon B. Black
48th Tennessee Infantry—Colonel William Milton Voorhees
49th Tennessee Infantry—Major David A. Lynn
53rd Tennessee Infantry—Lieutenant Colonel John R. White
1st Texas Sharpshooter Battalion—Major James Burnet

Evans's Brigade—Brigadier General Nathan George Evans
17th South Carolina Infantry—Colonel Fitz William McMasters

18th South Carolina Infantry—Colonel William H. Wallace
22nd South Carolina Infantry—Lieutenant Colonel James O'Connell
23rd South Carolina Infantry—Colonel Henry Laurens Benbow
26th South Carolina Infantry—Colonel Alexander Davis Smith
Holcombe South Carolina Legion—Lieutenant Colonel William James Crawley

Division Artillery

Fenner's Louisiana Battery—Captain Charles Erasmus Fenner
Macbeth South Carolina Artillery—Lieutenant B.A. Jeter
Culpeper's South Carolina Battery—Captain James Furman Culpeper

Loring's Division

Major General William Wing Loring

Adams's Brigade—Brigadier General John Adams
1st Confederate Infantry Battalion—Lieutenant Colonel George Hoke Forney
6th Mississippi Infantry—Colonel Robert Lowry
14th Mississippi—Lieutenant Colonel Washington L. Doss
15th Mississippi—Colonel Michael Farrell
20th Mississippi Infantry—Lieutenant Colonel William Newton Brown
23rd Mississippi Infantry—Colonel Joseph Morehead Wells
26th Mississippi Infantry—Lieutenant Colonel Francis Marion Boone
Lookout Tennessee Artillery—Captain Robert L. Barry

Buford's Brigade—Brigadier General Abraham Buford
27th Alabama Infantry—Colonel James Jackson
35th Alabama Infantry—Colonel Edward Goodwin
54th Alabama Infantry—Major T.H. Shackelford
55th Alabama Infantry—Colonel John Snodgrass
9th Arkansas Infantry—Colonel Isaac Leroy Dunlop
3rd Kentucky Infantry—Colonel Albert Petty Thompson
7th Kentucky Infantry—Colonel Edward Crossland
8th Kentucky Infantry—Lieutenant Colonel Absalom Redmond Shacklett
12th Louisiana Infantry—Colonel Thomas Moore Scott

3rd Missouri Cavalry Battalion (Dismounted)—Lieutenant Colonel D. Todd Samuels

Pointe Coupee Artillery—Captain Joseph Alcide Bouanchaud

Featherston's Brigade—Brigadier General Winfield Scott Featherston/ Colonel Jehu Amaziah Orr

3rd Mississippi Infantry—Major Samuel A. Dyer

22nd Mississippi Infantry—Lieutenant Colonel Hugh J. Reid

31st Mississippi Infantry—Lieutenant Colonel Maquis De Lafayette Stephens

33rd Mississippi Infantry—Colonel David Wiley Hurst

1st Mississippi Sharpshooter Battalion—Major James Monroe Stigler

Charpentier's Alabama Battery—Captain Stephen Charpentier

14th Mississippi Artillery Battalion (Company C)—Captain Jacob C. Culbertson

Walker's Division

Major General William Henry Talbot Walker

Ector's Brigade—Brigadier General Matthew D. Ector

40th Alabama Infantry Battalion—Major Thomas O. Stone

43rd Mississippi Infantry Sharpshooter Battalion—Captain M. Pounds

9th Texas Infantry—Lieutenant Colonel Miles Anderson Dillard

10th Texas Cavalry (Dismounted)—Lieutenant Colonel Cullin Redwine Earp

14th Texas Cavalry (Dismounted)—Colonel John Lafayette Camp

32nd Texas Cavalry (Dismounted)—Colonel Julius A. Andrews

McNally's Arkansas Battery—Lieutenant F.A. Moore

Gist's Brigade—Brigadier General States Rights Gist

8th Georgia Infantry Battalion—Captain Zachariah L. Watters

46th Georgia Infantry—Colonel Peyton H. Colquitt

16th South Carolina Infantry—Colonel James McCullough

24th South Carolina Infantry—Colonel Clement H. Stevens

Ferguson's South Carolina Battery—Captain T.B. Ferguson

Gregg's Brigade—Brigadier General John Gregg

3rd Tennessee Infantry—Colonel Calvin Harvey Walker

10th Tennessee Infantry—Lieutenant Colonel William Grace

30th Tennessee Infantry—Lieutenant Colonel James J. Turner
41st Tennessee Infantry—Colonel Robert Farquharson
50th Tennessee Infantry—Colonel Cyrus Alexandrian Sugg
1st Tennessee Infantry Battalion—Major Stephen H. Colms
7th Texas Infantry—Colonel Hiram Bronson Granbury
Bledsoe's Missouri Battery—Captain Hiram Miller Bledsoe

Wilson's Brigade—Colonel Claudius Charles Wilson
1st Georgia Sharpshooter Battalion—Major Arthur Shaaff
25th Georgia Infantry—Lieutenant Colonel Andrew Jackson Williams
29th Georgia Infantry—Colonel William Joshua Young
30th Georgia—Colonel Thomas Woodward Mangham
4th Louisiana Infantry Battalion—Lieutenant Colonel John McEnery
Martin's Georgia Battery—Lieutenant Evan P. Howell
Nelson's Independent Company of Georgia Cavalry—Captain T.M. Nelson

Cavalry Division

Brigadier General William Hicks Jackson

First Brigade—Brigadier General George Blake Cosby
1st Mississippi Cavalry—Colonel Richard Alexander Pinson
4th Mississippi Cavalry—Major James Lyons Burks Harris Harris
28th Mississippi Cavalry—Colonel Peter Burwell Starke
Adams's Mississippi Cavalry—Colonel William Wirt Adams
Ballentine's Mississippi Cavalry—Lieutenant Colonel William L. Maxwell
17th Mississippi Cavalry Battalion (State Troops)—Major Abner C. Steede
Clark's Missouri Battery—Captain Houston King

Second Brigade—Brigadier General John Wilkins Whitfield
1st Texas Legion—Lieutenant Colonel John Henry Broocks
3rd Texas Cavalry—Lieutenant Colonel Jiles Sanford Boggess Jr.
6th Texas Cavalry—Major John Mason "Jack" Wharton
9th Texas Cavalry—Colonel Dudley William Jones
Bridge's Cavalry Battalion—Major Henry W. Bridges

Escorts and Guards
7th Tennessee Cavalry, Company A—Captain W.F. Taylor

Independent Company Louisiana Cavalry—Captain Junius Y. Webb
4th Mississippi Cavalry, Company D—Captain James Ruffin

Reserve Artillery—Major William C. Preston
Columbus Georgia Battery—Captain Edward Croft
Durrive's Louisana Battery—Captain Edward Durrive Jr.
Palmetto South Carolina Artillery, Battery B—Captain John Waites

NOTES

INTRODUCTION

1. Shea and Winschel, *Vicksburg Is the Key*, 170–78.
2. Brinson, *Jackson*, 53–85; Skates, *Mississippi's Old Capitol*, 19–46; Historic Resources Inventory, MDAH.
3. Boman, "City of the Old South," 8; Historic Resources Inventory, MDAH.
4. "Professional and Business Directory."
5. Brinson, *Jackson*, 74–75; "Professional and Business Directory."
6. Brinson, *Jackson*, 72–74.
7. Bettersworth, *Mississippi in the Confederacy*, 26–27; Harrington, "Prayer for the New Born Republic."

CHAPTER 1

8. U.S. War Department, *War of the Rebellion*, series 1, vol. 24, 1:239. Hereinafter cited as OR; *Daily Mississippian*, May 5 and May 10, 1863; Johnston, *Narrative*, 172.
9. Davis, *Confederate General*, vol. 3, 193–97; Symonds, *Joseph E. Johnston*, 123–39.
10. Symonds, *Joseph E. Johnston*, 187–203; Winschel, *Triumph & Defeat*, vol. 2, 116–21.
11. OR, series 1, vol. 24, 2:239; Shea and Winschel, *Vicksburg Is the Key*, 124.
12. OR, series 1, vol. 24, 1:215–16, 239. No earthworks existed prior to the beginning of May, when Governor Pettus called on citizens to volunteer

their slaves to erect fortifications. A few days later, a large number of citizens also pitched in to erect these earthworks. Bearss, *Campaign for Vicksburg*, vol. 2, 308.

13. Winschel, *Fall of the Confederate Gibraltar*, 14.
14. Ballard, *Civil War in Mississippi*, 156–62.
15. OR, series 1, vol. 24, 1:785–87; Ballard, *Vicksburg*, 277. Thompson was killed on March 25, 1864, while leading troops in a raid by Forrest's cavalry in Kentucky. He was within sight of his home in Paducah, Kentucky. See http://explorekyhistory.ky.gov/items/show/22.
16. OR, series 1, vol. 24, 1:777, 786–87; Bearss and Grabau, *Battle of Jackson*, 23–25.
17. OR, series 1, vol. 24, 1:754; Grant, *Personal Memoirs*, vol. 1, 423.
18. OR, series 1, vol. 24, 1:754–55; OR, series 1, vol. 24, 3:312; Bradley, *Last Stand in the Carolinas*, 60. Frank Blair, commanding the second division in the XV corps, was accompanying the supply train.
19. Kraynek, *Letters to My Wife*, 64–65.
20. OR, series 1, vol. 24, 3:315; Bearss and Grabau, *Battle of Jackson*, 29–32.
21. OR, series 1, vol. 24, 3:881.
22. Fremantle, *Three Months in the Southern States*, 113, 116–17.
23. Wynne, *Hard Trip*, 106.
24. Goodloe, *Confederate Echoes*, 220.
25. Bearss, *Campaign for Vicksburg*, vol. 3, 976–77; Winschel, *Triumph & Defeat*, 122–24.
26. Warner, *Generals in Gray*, 34; Davis, *Confederate General*, 363–66.
27. Bearss, *Campaign for Vicksburg*, 1079.
28. OR, series 1, vol. 24, 1:227–28.
29. Taylor, *Reluctant Rebel*, 117–18; Carter, *Two Stars in the Southern Sky*, 180.
30. OR, series 1, vol. 24, 3: 960, 965–66; Bearss, *Campaign for Vicksburg*, 1085.
31. Bearss, *Campaign for Vicksburg*, 1079.
32. Warner, *Generals in Blue*, 441–44.
33. Winschel, *Triumph & Defeat*, 126–28.
34. French, *Two Wars*, 182; Bearss, *Campaign for Vicksburg*, 1127–38.

CHAPTER 2

35. OR, series 1, vol. 24, 3:460–61.
36. Ibid., 461–64; Mason, *Forty-Second Ohio Infantry*, 231.
37. Warner, *Generals in Blue*, 359–60.

38. OR, series 1, vol. 24, 3:475.
39. Ibid., 2:560, 574, 620–21.
40. Ibid., 574, 591.
41. Ibid., 620–21.
42. Warner, *Generals in Gray*, 333–34.
43. Rose, *Ross' Texas Brigade*, 109.
44. OR, series 1, vol. 24, 2:628, 639, 644.
45. *Confederate Veteran*, 1903, 23.
46. OR, series 1, vol. 24, 2:556.
47. Cuffel, *History of Durell's Battery*, 127, 142.
48. OR, series 1, vol. 24, 2:569.
49. Bearss and Grabau, *Battle of Jackson*, 63.
50. Edwards, *Condensed History*, 34.
51. Taylor, *Reluctant Rebel*, 119–20; French, *Two Wars*, 182.
52. Flood, Letter, 2.
53. OR, series 1, vol. 24, 1:245; *Charleston Mercury*, July 28, 1863; "Withers Family," 312–13.
54. OR, series 1, vol. 24, 1:245; Davis, *Confederate General*, vol. 4, 97–98.
55. Warner, *Generals in Gray*, 323–24; Mitchell, "Recollections."
56. Warner, *Generals in Gray*, 93–94.
57. Davis, *Confederate General*, vol. 1, 126–27.
58. Warner, *Generals in Gray*, 132, 294–95.
59. OR, series 1, vol. 24, 3:994–95.

Chapter 3

60. OR, series 1, vol. 24, 3:482, 485; OR, series 1, vol. 24, 2:521, 533–34, 556, 581; Reed, *Campaigns and Battles of the Twelfth Iowa*, 128.
61. Rose, *Ross' Texas Brigade*, 110; Hunter, "Sketch of the History of the Noxubee Troopers," 9.
62. OR, series 1, vol. 24, 2:581.
63. Kohl, *Prairie Boys Go to War*, 131.
64. OR, series 1, vol. 24, 2:581–84.
65. Adamson, *Brief History*, 30.
66. Sheppard, "Our Darkest Times," 79.
67. *History of the Forty-Sixth Indiana*, 66–67.
68. Tisdale Diary, July 7, 1863.
69. Lee, "Wagonmaster's Letter," 31.

70. Bentley, *History of the 77ᵗʰ Illinois*, 187.

71. Sears, *For Country, Cause & Leader*, 337.

72. Bilby, "Memoirs of Military Service," 27.

73. Street, Papers.

74. Cuffel, *History of Durell's Battery*, 143.

75. Reed, *Twelfth Regiment Iowa*, 128.

76. Ranlett, *History of the Thirty-Sixth Massachusetts*, 59.

77. OR, series 1, vol. 24, 2:577–78.

78. Ibid., 552, 556, 625, 630–36, 646.

79. Ibid., 3:491; Bearss and Grabau, *Battle of Jackson*, 72–73.

80. OR, series 1, vol. 24, 2:534–35; Winschel, *Triumph & Defeat*, vol. 2, 132. On one occasion, a projectile from the 32-pounder landed in a camp kettle of the Twelfth Iowa Infantry, ruining the dinner and the kettle but causing no additional injuries. Reed, *Twelfth Regiment Iowa*, 129.

81. OR, series 1, vol. 24, 2:578, 582; Bearss and Grabau, *Battle of Jackson*, 74–75.

82. OR, series 1, vol. 24, 2:584–85.

83. Ibid., 592.

84. Ibid., 594. Following this action, Osterhaus went to the front and sat down behind the works facing the Confederate trenches and said, "I takes a front seat." "Just then," according to a soldier in the Seventy-seventh Illinois, "a shell came howling overhead and exploded behind the general. Quick as thought he whirled around and taking a seat on the other side of the trench, he said, 'I takes a pack seat.' The men hailed the movement and the remark with cheers and roars of laughter." This incident may have contributed to persistent (and false) reports of Osterhaus's death during the siege. Townsend, *Yankee Warhorse*, 117–18.

85. Bearss and Grabau, *Battle of Jackson*, 75–76; Crooke, *Twenty-First Regiment*, 112–13.

86. Ranlett, *History of the Thirty-sixth Massachusetts*, 60.

87. OR, series 1, vol. 24, 2: 557–58, 561, 563.

88. Ibid., 558, 561; Cuffel, *History of Durell's Battery*, 146; Albert, *History of the Forty-Fifth Regiment*, 72.

89. OR, series 1, vol. 24, 2:558.

90. Ibid., 522, 534–35; OR, series 1, vol. 24, 3:496, 508.

91. Bearss and Grabau, *Battle of Jackson*, 79.

92. OR, series 1, vol. 24, 2:609.

93. Ibid., 597, 600, 658.

94. Ibid., 556, 558, 566. This line is located near present-day Morningside Street and Moody Street, a short distance south of Fortification Street.
95. Sears, *For Country, Cause & Leader*, 338–39.
96. Ibid., 362; OR, series 1, vol. 24, 2:566.
97. Ibid., 561. Millsaps College occupies a portion of the ridge on which Smith's troops were positioned.
98. Davis, *Diary of a Confederate Soldier*, 79–80.

CHAPTER 4

99. Ranstead, *True Story and History*; Jones, *Christ in the Camp*, 551.
100. OR, series 1, vol. 24, 2:502–03.
101. Bearss and Grabau, *Battle of Jackson*, 84; Soman and Byrne, *Jewish Colonel in the Civil War*, 301.
102. OR, series 1, vol. 24, 2: 506–09.
103. Ibid., 597–98, 602.
104. Warner, *Generals in Blue*, 275–76.
105. OR, series 1, vol. 17, 1:325; Cozzens, *Darkest Days of the War*, 280–90.
106. Pugh Papers; Johns, *Personal Recollections of Early Decatur*, 128–29.
107. OR, series 1, vol. 24, 3:503–04; OR, series 1, vol. 24, 2:603–07. The position held by Hovey's division was at the time known as Winter's Woods. A portion of Hovey's earthworks are preserved in Battlefield Park.
108. OR, series 1, vol. 24, 2:603–07; Hughes, *Pride of the Confederate Artillery*, 8–9, 105.
109. Davis, *Confederate General*, vol. 1, 2–5; Warner, *Generals in Gray*, 1–3.
110. Holder, *William Winans*, 186, 213, 220.
111. Ranstead Diary, 6; OR, series 1, vol. 24, 2:604.
112. OR, series 1, vol. 24, 2:604–08, 654–57.
113. Hughes, *Pride of the Confederate Artillery*, 112–13.
114. OR, series 1, vol. 24, 2:605.
115. Hughes, *Pride of the Confederate Artillery*, 114.
116. Sheppard, "Our Darkest Times," 85; OR, series 1, vol. 24, 2:604.
117. OR, series 1, vol. 24, 2:604–08, 654–57; Reddick, *Seventy-seven Years in Dixie*, 39; *Past and Present of La Salle County*, 121. A street just off of Gallatin Street near downtown Jackson is named for Earl.
118. Stuart, *Iowa Colonels*, 97–108; *Portrait and Biographical Album*, 235.
119. Renaldo Pugh Letter, July 13, 1863.
120. Dougan, "Hermann Hirsch and the Siege of Jackson," 26.

121. OR, series 1, vol. 24, 2: 656. "Harry" Maury was twice court-martialed for drunkenness but was acquitted both times. Allardice, *Confederate Colonels*, 257.

122. OR, series 1, vol. 24, 3:1001; Davis, *Diary of a Confederate Soldier*, 80.

123. *New York Times*, June 20, 1885; Moran, "His Heart's Blood."

124. OR, series 1, vol. 24, 2:575, 598.

125. Ibid., 603–04.

126. Isaac Pugh Letter, July 29, 1863.

127. Renaldo Pugh Letter, July 26, 1863.

128. Hobart, "Story of Vicksburg and Jackson," 15–21; Warner, *Generals in Blue*, 270.

129. Renaldo Pugh Letter, July 13, 1863; Hughes, *Pride of the Confederate Artillery*, 117.

130. OR, series 1, vol. 24, 3:509–10; 1002–03.

131. Allardice, *Confederate Colonels*, 412; Bellware, "Colonel Leon Von Zinken."

132. OR, series 1, vol. 24, 2:655; Sheppard, "Our Darkest Times," 86.

133. OR, series 1, vol. 24, 3:1003.

134. Crowson and Brogden, *Bloody Banners and Barefoot Boys*, 40; *Story of the Fifty-fifth*, 259.

135. Jones, *Reminiscences of the Twenty-Second Iowa*, 45.

136. Hughes, *Pride of the Confederate Artillery*, 117.

Chapter 5

137. OR, series 1, vol. 24, 2: 563–65, 571, 590–91, 657.

138. Ferrell, *Holding the Line*, 137; Armstrong Letters, July 14, 1863; Jones, *Reminiscences*, 45–46.

139. OR, series 1, vol. 24, 3:510; OR, series 1, vol. 24, 2:559–60; Cuffel, *History of Durell's Battery*, 148.

140. Johnston, *Narrative*, 208; Bearss and Grabau, *Battle of Jackson*, 90.

141. OR, series 1, vol. 24, 2:554–55; OR, series 1, vol. 24, 3:1015–16; *Roster and Record*, 318.

142. OR, series 1, vol. 24, 2:653–54; OR, series 1, vol. 24, 3:513.

143. Crabb, *All Afire to Fight*, 143; OR, series 1, vol. 24, 3:1016.

144. OR, series 1, vol. 24, 2:595, 606.

145. Ibid., 555, 567, 572, 648–49.

146. Ibid., 567, 572–73; Mettendorf, *Between Triumph and Disaster*, 59.

147. OR, series 1, vol. 24, 2: 648–49.

148. Alexander, *History of the Ninety-Seventh Regiment*, 7.

149. Zollinger, "I Take My Pen in Hand," 166; OR, series 1, vol. 24, 2:641.

150. OR, series 1, vol. 24, 2:645–50; Wright, *History of the Sixth Iowa Infantry*, 207–08.

151. OR, series 1, vol. 24, 2:536–37; Mead, *Land Between Two Rivers*, 50–52; *Memphis Daily Appeal*, September 24, 1863.

152. Warner, *Generals in Blue*, 58–59; Bearss, *Campaign for Vicksburg*, vol. 3, 1079, 1129.

153. OR, series 1, vol. 24, 2:552; Davis, *Confederate General*, vol. 1, 35–36; Kohl, *Prairie Boys Go to War*, 133.

154. OR, series 1, vol. 24, 2:577.

155. Ibid., 577–79, 588–89; *Confederate Veteran*, vol. 4, 437.

156. *Papers Relating to Foreign Affairs*, 606, 679–81. As a diplomat, Lyons is credited with helping avoid war between the United States and Great Britain in 1861 by securing the release of James Mason and John Slidell, two Confederate envoys, who had been seized aboard the British mail steamer *Trent*.

157. OR, series 1, vol. 24, 2:579.

158. Warner, *Generals in Blue*, 571–72.

159. *Daily Cleveland*, June 22, 1866.

160. OR, series 1, vol. 24, 2:551–54, 618–19; Bennett and Tillery, *Struggle for the Life of the Republic*, 117.

161. OR, series 1, vol. 24, 2: 552–53, 618–19; *Canton American Citizen*, September 19, 1863.

162. Bee, "Civil War Diary of John T. Buegel," 512; OR, series 1, vol. 24, 2:579, 661; *Memphis Daily Appeal*, September 24, 1863.

163. Willison, *Reminiscences of a Boy's Service with the 76th Ohio*, 65; OR, series 1, vol. 24, 2:618–19.

Chapter 6

164. OR, series 1, vol. 24, 3:1008; Meyer, *Iowa Valor*, 253; Williams, *Chicago's Battery Boys*, 148; Bringhurst and Swigart, *History of the Forty-Sixth Regiment Indiana*, 69.

165. *History of the Thirty-Fifth Regiment Massachusetts Volunteers*, 147–48; Parker, *History of the 51st Regiment*, 362.

166. Jackson City Minutes, 9.

167. OR, series 1, vol. 24, 2:530–32.

168. Parker, *History of the 51st Regiment* 364–65.
169. Duke, *History of the Fifty-Third Regiment Ohio Volunteer Infantry*, 112; OR, series 1, vol. 24, 3:524–25.
170. OR, series 1, vol. 24, 2:536.
171. OR, series 1, vol. 24, 3: 531; Sansing and Waller, *History of the Mississippi Governor's Mansion*, 53; OR, series 1, vol. 24, 2:536–37; OR, series 1, vol. 24, 3:522.
172. Bearss and Grabau, *Battle of Jackson*, 100–01.
173. Wilson and Fiske, *Appleton's Cyclodaedia of American Biography*, vol. 2, 621.
174. OR, series 1, vol. 24, 2:623–26; OR, series 1, vol. 24, 3:1018; Bearss and Grabau, *Battle of Jackson*, 101.
175. Reed, *Twelfth Regiment Iowa*, 132.
176. Bearss and Grabau, *Battle of Jackson*, 102–03.
177. OR, series 1, vol. 24, 2:541–42; Elliott Diary, July 17, 1863.
178. OR, series 1, vol. 24, 2:599; Winschel, *Civil War Diary of a Common Soldier*, 68.
179. OR, series 1, vol. 24, 2:530–37.
180. Ibid., 537; Ballard, *Civil War in Mississippi*, 171.

CHAPTER 7

181. Howell, "Most Appalling Disaster."
182. OR, series 1, vol. 24, 1:754; Freemantle, *Three Months in the Southern States*, 110.
183. McCain, *Story of Jackson*, 195.
184. Armstrong Letters, July 14, 1863.
185. *Canton American Citizen*, September 19, 1863.
186. Tisdale Diary, July 17, 1863.
187. Roper, *Now the Drum of War*, 243.
188. Williams, *Chicago's Battery Boys*, 149.
189. Howell, *Chimneyville*, 57.
190. Pierson, Diary and Letters of Thomas Buchanan Linn, 16th O.V.I., July 17, 1863.
191. Swan, *Chicago's Irish Legion*, 79.
192. *Boston Daily*, July 30, 1863.
193. *Houston Tri-Weekly*, September 23, 1863.

194. *Charleston Mercury*, July 31, 1863; author interview with McQuade descendant, Salt Lake City.
195. Howell, *To Live and Die in Dixie*, 227–28. It was in this newspaper account that the term "Chimneyville" first appeared.
196. *Memphis Daily Appeal*, August 21, 1863.
197. *Proceedings at the Forty-Sixth Grand Annual Communication of the M.W. Grand Lodge*, 4–6.
198. Elder Diary, 40, 47.
199. Jackson City Minutes, 10.
200. "Professional and Business Directory," 1860.
201. *Jackson Daily Clarion*, January 9, 1866.
202. Sanders, *Images of America: Jackson's North State Street*, 9–24.
203. Howell, *Chimneyville*, 70.
204. Von Seutter Digital Collection, MDAH.

Bibliography

Books

Adamson, A.P. *Brief History of the Thirtieth Georgia Regiment*. Griffin, GA: Mills Printing Co., 1912.

Albert, Allen D. *History of the Forty-Fifth Regiment Pennsylvania Veteran Volunteer Infantry, 1861–1865*. Williamsport, PA: Frit Publishing Co., 1912.

Alexander, John D. *History of the Ninety-Seventh Regiment of Indiana Volunteer Infantry*. Terre Haute, IN: Moore & Lanorn, 1891.

Allardice, Bruce S. *Confederate Colonels: A Biographical Register*. Columbia: University of Missouri Press, 2008.

Ballard, Michael B. *The Civil War in Mississippi: Major Campaigns and Battles*. Jackson: University Press of Mississippi, 2011.

———. *Pemberton: A Biography*. Jackson: University Press of Mississippi, 1991.

———. *Vicksburg: The Campaign That Opened the Mississippi*. Chapel Hill: University of North Carolina Press, 2004.

Barron, S.B. *The Lone Star Defenders: A Chronicle of the Third Texas Cavalry, Ross' Brigade*. New York: Neale Publishing Company, 1908.

Bearss, Edwin C. *The Campaign for Vicksburg*. 3 vols. Dayton, OH: Morningside House, Inc., 1986.

Bearss, Edwin C., and Warren Grabau. *The Battle of Jackson, the Siege of Jackson and Three Other Post-Vicksburg Actions*. Jackson, MS: Gateway Press, Inc., 1981.

Bennett, Stewart, and Barbara Tillery, eds. *The Struggle for the Life of the Republic: A Civil War Narrative by Brevet Major Charles Dana Miller, 76th Ohio Volunteer Infantry*. Kent, OH: Kent State University Press, 2004.

Bentley, W.H. *History of the 77th Illinois Volunteer Infantry, September 2, 1862–July 10, 1865*. Peoria, IL: Edward Hine, Printer, 1883.

Bettersworth, John K. *Mississippi in the Confederacy: As They Saw It*. Baton Rouge: Louisiana State University Press, 1961.

Bradley, Mark L. *Last Stand in the Carolinas: The Battle of Bentonville*. Campbell, CA: Savas Publishing Company, 1996.

Bringhurst, Thomas H., and Frank Swigart. *History of the Forty-Sixth Regiment Indiana Volunteer Veteran Infantry*. Logansport, IN: Wilson, Humphreys & Co., 1888.

Brinson, Carroll. *Jackson: A Special Kind of Place*. Jackson, MS: Hederman Brothers Printing, 1977.

Carter, Davis Blake. *Two Stars in the Southern Sky: General John Gregg C.S.A. and Mollie*. Spartanburg, SC: Reprint Company, 2001.

Cogswell, Leander. *A History of the Eleventh New Hampshire Regiment Volunteer Infantry*. Concord, NH: Republican Press Association, 1891.

Confederate Veteran Magazine, 1893–1932. Wilmington, NC: Broadfoot Publishing Company, 1987. Reprint.

Cozzens, Peter. *The Darkest Days of the War: The Battles of Iuka & Corinth*. Chapel Hill: University of North Carolina Press, 1997.

Crabb, Martha L. *All Afire to Fight: The Untold Tale of the Civil War's Ninth Texas Cavalry*. New York: Avon Books, 2000.

Crooke, George. *The Twenty-First Regiment of Iowa Volunteer Infantry: A Narrative of Its Experience in Active Service*. Milwaukee, WI: King, Fowle & Co., 1891.

Cross, C. Wallace. *Cry Havoc: A History of the 49th Tennessee Volunteer Infantry Regiment, 1861–1865*. Franklin, TN: Hillsboro Press, 2004.

Crowson, Noel, and John V. Brogden, eds. *Bloody Banners and Barefoot Boys: A History of the 27th Regiment Alabama Infantry, CSA*. Sippensburg, PA: Burd Street Press, 1997.

Cuffel, Charles A. *History of Durell's Battery in the Civil War*. Philadelphia: Craig Finley & Co., 1903.

Davis, William C. *Breckinridge: Statesman Soldier Symbol*. Baton Rouge: Louisiana State University Press, 1974.

———. *The Confederate General*. 6 vols. Washington, D.C.: National Historical Society, 1991.

———, ed. *Diary of a Confederate Soldier: John S. Jackman of the Orphan Brigade*. Columbia: University of South Carolina Press, 1990.

Davis, William C. *The Orphan Brigade: The Kentucky Confederates Who Couldn't Go Home*. Baton Rouge: Louisiana State University Press, 1980.

Drake, Edwin L., ed. *The Annals of the Army of Tennessee and Early Western History*. Vol. 1. Nashville, TN: A.D. Haynes, 1878.

Duke, John K. *History of the Fifty-Third Regiment Ohio Volunteer Infantry*. Portsmouth, OH: Blade Printing Company, 1900.

Edwards, William Henry. *A Condensed History of Seventeenth Regiment S.C.V. C.S.A.: From Its Organization to the Close of the War*. Columbia: Press of the R.L. Bryan Co. (University of South Carolina Library, Digital Collections), 1908.

Ferrell, Robert H., ed. *Holding the Line: The Third Tennessee Infantry, 1861–1864*. Kent, OH: Kent State University Press, 1994.

Fremantle, Arthur. *Three Months in the Southern States: April–June 1863*. Edinburgh, Scotland: William Blackwood and Sons, 1863.

French, Samuel G. *Two Wars: An Autobiography of Gen. Samuel G. French*. Huntington, WV: Blue Acorn Press, 1999. First published 1901 by Confederate Veteran.

Goodloe, Albert T. *Confederate Echoes: A Soldier's Personal Story of Life in the Confederate Army from the Mississippi to the Carolinas*. Washington, D.C.: Zenger Publishing Co., 1983.

Grant, Ulysses S. *Personal Memoirs of U.S. Grant in Two Volumes*. New York: Charles L. Webster Company, 1885.

Hart, E.J. *History of the Fortieth Illinois Infantry*. Cincinnati, OH: H.S. Bosworth, 1864.

History of the Forty-Sixth Regiment Indiana Volunteer Infantry. Logansport, IN: Wilson, Humphreys & Co., 1888.

History of the Thirty-Fifth Regiment Massachusetts Volunteers, 1862–1865, with a Roster. Boston: Mills, Knight & Co., 1884.

Holder, Ray. *William Winans: Methodist Leader in Antebellum Mississippi*. Jackson: University Press of Mississippi, 1977.

Hopkins, William P. *The Seventh Regiment Rhode Island Volunteers in the Civil War, 1862–1865*. Providence, RI: Snow & Farnham Printers, 1903.

Howell, H. Grady, Jr. *Chimneyville: "Likenesses" of Early Days in Jackson, Mississippi*. Jackson, MS: Chickasaw Bayou Press, 2007.

———. *Going to Meet the Yankees: A History of the "Bloody Sixth" Mississippi Infantry, C.S.A.* Jackson, MS: Chickasaw Bayou Press, 1981.

———. *To Live and Die in Dixie: A History of the Third Regiment Mississippi Volunteer Infantry, C.S.A.* Jackson, MS: Chickasaw Bayou Press, 1991.

Hughes, Nathaniel Cheairs, Jr. *The Pride of the Confederate Artillery: The Washington Artillery in the Army of Tennessee*. Baton Rouge: Louisiana State University Press, 1997.

Johns, Jane Martin. *Personal Recollections of Early Decatur, Abraham Lincoln, Richard J. Oglesby and the Civil War*. Decatur, IL: Decatur Chapter Daughters of the American Revolution, 1912.

Johnston, Joseph Eggleston. *Narrative of Military Operations Directed During the Late War Between the States*. New York: D. Appleton and Company, 1874.

Jones, J. William. *Christ in the Camp*. Akron, OH: B.F. Johnson & Co., 1887.

Jones, S.C. *Reminiscences of the Twenty-Second Iowa Volunteer Infantry*. Reprint edition, Iowa City, IA: Camp Pope Bookshop, 1993. Originally published in 1907.

Kraynek, Sharon L.D., ed. *Letters to My Wife: A Civil War Diary from the Western Front*. Apollo, PA: Closson Press, 1995.

Kohl, Rhonda M. *The Prairie Boys Go to War: The Fifth Illinois Cavalry, 1861–1865*. Carbondale: Southern Illinois University Press, 2013.

Lowe, Richard, ed. *A Texas Cavalry Officer's Civil War: The Diary and Letters of James C. Bates*. Baton Rouge: Louisiana State University Press, 1999.

Marszalek, John F. *Sherman: A Soldier's Passion for Order*. New York: Free Press, 1993.

Mason, Frank H. *The Forty-Second Ohio Infantry: A History of the Organization and Services of That Regiment in the War of the Rebellion*. Cleveland, OH: Cobb, Andrews & Co., Publishers, 1876.

McCain, William D. *The Story of Jackson: A History of the Capital of Mississippi, 1821–1951*. Vol. 1. Jackson, MS: J.F. Hyer Publishing Company, 1953.

Mead, Carol Lynn. *The Land Between Two Rivers: Madison County, Mississippi*. Canton, MS: Friends of the Madison County–Canton Public Library, 1987.

Mettendorf, Ernest. *Between Triumph and Disaster: The History of the 46th New York Infantry, 1861 to 1865*. Self-published, 2012.

Meyer, Steve. *Iowa Valor*. Garrison, IA: Meyer Publishing Company, 1994.

Moore, Frank. *The Rebellion Record: A Diary of American Events*. Vol. 7. New York: D. Van Nostrand, 1864.

Papers Relating to Foreign Affairs, Accompanying the Annual Message of the President to the Second Session Thirty-Eighth Congress, Part II. Washington, D.C.: Government Printing Office, 1865.

Parker, Thomas H. *History of the 51st Regiment of P.V. and V.V., from its Organization, at Camp Curtin, Harrisburg, Pa., in 1861, to its Being Mustered out of the United States Service at Alexandria, Va., July 27th, 1865*. Philadelphia: King & Baird Printers, 1869.

The Past and Present of La Salle County, Illinois. Chicago: H.F. Kett & Co., 1877.

Portrait & Biographical Album of Fayette County Iowa. Chicago: Lake City Publishing Co., 1891.

Proceedings at the Forty-Sixth Grand Annual Communication of the M.W. Grand Lodge of Ancient Free and Accepted Masons of the State of Mississippi. Jackson, MS: Daily Clarion Book and Job Office, 1864.

Ranlett, S. Alonzo. *History of the Thirty-Sixth Regiment Massachusetts Volunteers, 1862–1865*. Boston: Press of Rockwell and Churchill, 1884.

Ranstead, H.E. *A True Story and History of the Fifty-Third Regiment, Illinois Veteran Volunteer Infantry*. Originally published in 1910. Accessed via http://civilwar.illinoisgenweb.org/scrapbk/ransteaddiary.html.

Reddick, Henry W. *Seventy-seven Years in Dixie: The Boys in Gray of 61–65*. Santa Rosa, FL: H.W. Reddick, 1910.

Reed, Major David W. *Campaigns and Battles of the Twelfth Regiment Iowa Veteran Volunteer Infantry*. Evanston, IL, 1903.

Roper, Robert. *Now the Drum of War: Walt Whitman and His Brother in the Civil War*. New York: Walker Publishing Company, 2008.

Rose, Victor M. *Ross' Texas Brigade: Being a Narrative of Events Connected with Its Service in the Late War Between the States*. Louisville, KY: Courier-Journal Book and Job Rooms, 1881.

Roster and Record of Iowa Soldiers in the War of the Rebellion. Vol. 1. Des Moines, IA: Adjutant General's Office, 1908.

Sanders, Todd. *Images of America: Jackson's North State Street*. Charleston, SC: Arcadia Publishing, 2009.

Sansing, David G., and Carroll Waller. *A History of the Mississippi Governor's Mansion*. Jackson: University Press of Mississippi, 1977.

Scott, Wm. Forse. *The Story of a Cavalry Regiment: The Career of the Fourth Iowa Veteran Volunteers from Kansas to Georgia, 1861–1865*. Iowa City, IA: Camp Pope Bookshop, 1992. First published 1893 by G.P. Putnam's Sons.

Sears, Stephen W. *For Country, Cause & Leader: The Civil War Journal of Charles B. Haydon*. New York: Ticknor & Fields, 1993.

Shea, William L., and Terrence J. Winschel. *Vicksburg Is the Key: The Struggle for the Mississippi River*. Lincoln: University of Nebraska Press, 2003.

Sherman, William Tecumseh. *Memoirs of General W.T. Sherman*. New York: Library of America, 1990.

Skates John Ray. *Mississippi's Old Capitol: Biography of a Building*. Jackson: Mississippi Department of Archives and History, 1990.

Smith, David M., ed. *Compelled to Appear in Print: The Vicksburg Manuscript of General John C. Pemberton*. Cincinnati, OH: Ironclad Publishing, 1999.

Soman, Jean Powers, and Frank L. Byrne, eds. *A Jewish Colonel in the Civil War: Marcus M. Spiegel of the Ohio Volunteers*. Lincoln: University of Nebraska Press, 1985.

The Story of the Fifty-fifth Regiment of Illinois Volunteer Infantry in the Civil War, 1861–1865, By a Committee of the Regiment. Huntington, WV: Blue Acorn Press, 1993. First published 1887 by W.J. Coulter.

Stuart, A.A. *Iowa Colonels and Regiments, Being a History of Iowa Regiments*. Des Moines, IA: Mills & Co., 1865.

Swan, James B. *Chicago's Irish Legion: The 90th Illinois Volunteers in the Civil War*. Carbondale: Southern Illinois University Press, 2009.

Symonds, Craig L. *Joseph E. Johnston: A Civil War Biography*. New York: W.W. Norton & Company, 1992.

Taylor, F. Jay, ed. *Reluctant Rebel: The Secret Diary of Robert Patrick, 1861–1865*. Baton Rouge: Louisiana State University Press, 1987.

Townsend, Mary Bobbitt. *Yankee Warhorse: A Biography of Major General Peter Osterhaus*. Columbia: University of Missouri Press, 2010.

U.S. War Department. *The War of the Rebellion: A Compilation of the Official Records of the Union and Confederate Armies*. 128 vols. Washington, D.C.: Government Printing Office, 1880–1901.

Warner, Ezra J. *Generals in Blue: Lives of the Union Commanders*. Baton Rouge: Louisiana State University Press, 1986.

———. *Generals in Gray: Lives of the Confederate Commanders*. Baton Rouge: Louisiana State University Press, 1989.

Williams, Richard Brady. *Chicago's Battery Boys: The Chicago Mercantile Battery in the Civil War's Western Theater*. New York: Savas Beatie, 2005.

Willison, Charles A. *Reminiscences of A Boy's Service with the 76th Ohio*. Menasha, WI: George Banta Publishing Company, 1908.

Wilson, James Grant, and John Fiske, eds. *Appleton's Cyclopaedia of American Biography*. Vol. 2. New York: D. Appleton and Co., 1888.

Winschel, Terrence J. *Triumph & Defeat: The Vicksburg Campaign*. Vol. 2. New York: Savas Publishing Company, 2006.

———. *Vicksburg: Fall of the Confederate Gibraltar*. Abilene, TX: McWhiney Foundation Press, 1999.

———, ed. *The Civil War Diary of a Common Soldier: William Wiley of the 77th Illinois Infantry*. Baton Rouge: Louisiana State University Press, 2001.

Wright, Henry H. *A History of the Sixth Iowa Infantry*. Iowa City: State Historical Society of Iowa, 1923.

Wynne, Ben. *A Hard Trip: A History of the 15th Mississippi Infantry, CSA*. Macon, GA: Mercer University Press, 2003.

Yeary, Mamie, ed. *Reminiscences of the Boys in Gray, 1861–1865.* Vol. 1. Dallas, TX: Smith & Lamar Publishing House, 1912.

PAPERS AND JOURNAL AND MAGAZINE ARTICLES

Bee, William G., trans. "The Civil War Diary of John T. Buegel, Union Soldier." *Missouri Historical Review* 40, no. 4 (1946).

Bellware, Daniel A. "Colonel Leon Von Zinken, Commandant of the Post at Columbus, Georgia." 2006. http://cvacwrt.tripod.com/zinken.html.

Bilby, Joseph G., ed. "Memoirs of Military Service." *Military Images Magazine* (September–October 1981), 27.

Boman, Martha. "A City of the Old South: Jackson, Mississippi, 1850–1860." *Journal of Mississippi History* 15 (1953), 1–32.

Dougan, Michael B. "Hermann Hirsch and the Siege of Jackson." *Journal of Mississippi History* 53, no. 1 (February 1991), Mississippi Historical Society.

Evans, E. Chris. "Return to Jackson: Finishing Stroke to the Vicksburg Campaign." *Blue & Gray Magazine* 12, no. 6, 8–63.

Hills, Colonel Parker. "Jackson's Civil War Landmarks," *Guard Detail* 4, no. 2 (February–April 1997), 5–9.

Howell, H. Grady, Jr. "The Most Appalling Disaster: Jackson Mississippi's Arsenal Explosion, November 5, 1862." 2002. http://battleofraymond. org/howell.htm.

Hunter, Joseph J. "A Sketch of the History of the Noxubee Troopers, First Mississippi Cavalry, Company F." MDAH.

Lee, George R., ed. "The Wagonmaster's Letter." *Civil War Times Illustrated* (March 1998), 30–33.

Moran, Rick. "His Heart's Blood Has Written Upon the Flag He Loved So Well." May 28, 2012. www.americanthinker.com.

"Professional and Business Directory of the City of Jackson." J.L. Power Collection, MDAH.

Sheppard, Jonathan C. "'This Seems to Be Our Darkest Times': The Florida Brigade in Mississippi, June–July 1863." *Florida Historical Quarterly* 85, no. 1 (Summer 2006), 64–90.

"The Withers Family of Stafford, Fauquier, &c." *Virginia Magazine of History and Biography* 6, no. 3 (January 1899), 309–13.

Zollinger, Vivian, ed. "'I Take My Pen in Hand,' Civil War Letters from Owen County, Indiana, Soldiers." *Indiana Magazine of History* 93, no. 2 (June 1997), 111–96.

Letters, Diaries, Memoirs and Papers

Armstrong, Lieutenant J.M. Letters, Lookout (TN) Artillery, http://genealogytrails.com/tenn/hamilton/chattanoogaletters ltarmstrongindexpage.htm.

Elder, Bishop William Henry. Diary, 1862–1865. Courtesy Catholic Diocese of Jackson.

Elliott, George. Diary, 97th Indiana Infantry, http://civilwarindiana.com.

Flood, John H. Letter, July 14, 1863. Michigan State University Archives & Historical Collections, Mrs. Earl Tooker Papers.

Harrington, Whitfield. "Prayer for the New Born Republic." MDAH Subject Files.

Hobart, Edwin L. "A Story of Vicksburg and Jackson." 1909, VNMP.

Jackson City Minutes. August 7, 1863. MDAH Subject Files.

Mitchell, Samuel. "Recollections," *Pulaski (TN) Citizen*, 1887. MDAH Historic Preservation Division Files.

Pierson, John M., trans. Diary and Letters of Thomas Buchanan Linn, 16th O.V.I., MDAH Historic Preservation Division Files.

Pugh, Isaac C. Collection, University of California, Riverside Libraries, Special Collections & Archives.

Street, John Kennedy Papers, 9th Texas Infantry, University of North Carolina at Chapel Hill.

Taylor, William. Letters, 100th Pennsylvania Infantry, VNMP.

Tisdale, Henry W. Diary, 35th Massachusetts Infantry. Courtesy Mark F. Farrell.

Von Seutter, Elisaeus Digital Photograph Collection, MDAH.

Williams, Enoch Pearson. "A Quaker Goes to War Against Slavery: The Limited Diary of Enoch Pearson Williams, Co. H, 8th Iowa Infantry," VNMP.

Newspapers

Boston Daily
Canton (MS) American Citizen
Charleston Mercury
Daily Cleveland
Daily Mississippian
Houston Tri-Weekly Telegraph
Jackson (MS) Daily Clarion
Macon (GA) Telegraph
Memphis (TN) Daily Appeal
New York Times
Semi-weekly Mississippian
Weekly Mississippian

INDEX

About the Author

Jim Woodrick is a native of Meridian, Mississippi, and a graduate of Millsaps College in Jackson. Since 1997, he has been on the staff of the Mississippi Department of Archives and History, where he worked for many years as the Civil War sites historian. In that capacity, he participated in a number of studies, battlefield acquisition projects and interpretive work with the National Park Service, the Civil War Trust and a number of battlefield preservation organizations in Mississippi. He is currently serving as director of the MDAH Historic Preservation Division.

A lifelong student of the Civil War, Jim has participated in living history events as a Civil War reenactor and is an active member of the Jackson Civil War Round Table and a member of the Historians of the Western Theater organization. He and his wife, Mary Margaret, live in Ridgeland, Mississippi.

Visit us at
www.historypress.net

....

This title is also available as an e-book

www.ingramcontent.com/pod-product-compliance
Lightning Source LLC
Chambersburg PA
CBHW060805100426
42813CB00004B/947